WA 1331272 3

D1439526

049800

WEB DESIGN INDEX

Compiled by Günter Beer

THE PEPIN PRESS / AGILE RABBIT EDITIONS
AMSTERDAM AND SINGAPORE

With special thanks to Magda Garcia Massana and Xavi Colomina from
LocTeam S.L., Barcelona.

The Publishers of this book did their utmost to comply with all legal
requirements. However, anyone who may claim any rights in respect to the
contents of this book who believes that, despite these endeavours, his or
her rights are infringed, is requested to immediately contact the Publishers.
In the event the Publishers agree with the objections raised, the Publishers
will take all reasonable action to satisfy this person's claim.

All rights reserved
Copyright © 2000 Pepin van Roojen

Compiled and edited by Günter Beer
(www.webdesignindex.org)
compilation and concept copyright © 2000 Günter Beer

Cover and page design by Pepin van Roojen

Introduction by Günter Beer and Pepin van Roojen
Translations by LocTeam, Barcelona (Spanish, French and Italian), Gabriela
Honecker and Sebastian Viebahn, Cologne (German), and Mitaka, Leeds
(Japanese).

ISBN 90 5768 018 1

Agile Rabbit Editions
c/o The Pepin Press BV
P.O. Box 10349
1001 EH Amsterdam
The Netherlands

Tel +31 20 4202021
Fax +31 20 4201152
mail@pepinpress.com
www.pepinpress.com

Printed in Singapore

13312723

Web Design Index

In this first edition of the Web Design Index, 1,002 outstanding web pages are presented. With each page, the URL is indicated, and, when known to us, the name of the designer and his or her email address.

In the inside back cover, you will find a CD-ROM containing all pages, arranged according to their location in this book. You can view them on your monitor with a minimum of loading time, and access the internet (provided you have a connection) to explore the selected site in full. On the CD, you will find a MacIntosh and a Windows folder. Mac users can navigate directly from the corresponding page number. For Windows, each site is contained in a folder with several files. Look for the 'index', 'start', or 'default' file to access your choice. Should this present problems, key in the URL in your internet browser.

The screenshots in the index and the CD were taken with MacIntosh versions of Explorer 4.5 and Netscape 4.6, allowing standard typography, Java and Shockwave. These capabilities are incorporated in modern browsers, and can be dowloaded from the internet for free.

The principal criteria on which this index's selection is based are design quality and innovation, and the page's effectiveness. Web design can range from single-page sites with simple, text-only layouts, to snazzy and complicated structures featuring the latest capabilities. Both have their particular purpose, and both can be beautiful and effective. Therefore, both, and all styles in between, are featured in this index. As design is the focal point of this index, no attempt has been made to classify the selection, other than arrange and group the designs on principal colour.

The internet is a medium subject to unprecedented change, and pages designed only one or two years ago may already look old fashioned. Likewise, some pages may have changed, or even disappeared from the net, since we selected them for the index. Nevertheless, this index should give an as accurate as possible overview of the state of the art in web design.

We would like to thank the following for their help in putting this edition of the Web Design Index together: coolhomepages.com, shift.co.jp, Yahoo's section on web designers, and Macromedia's 'shocked site of the day' (www.shockwave.com).

The following symbols have been used in this book:

◁꜀ site contains sound

▣□ site contains animation/video

Submissions

The Web Design Index will be published on an annual basis. Designs can be submitted for consideration for the next edition of the Web Design Index by mailing them via www.webdesignindex.org.

The Pepin Press/Agile Rabbit Editions

The Pepin Press/Agile Rabbit Editions publishes a wide range of books and CD-ROMs with visual reference material and ready-to-use images for designers, for internet applications as well as high-resolution printed media. For more information visit www.pepinpress.com.

Index de modèles de sites Web

Cette première édition de l'Index de modèles de sites Web vous présente 1.002 pages Web exceptionnelles. L'adresse URL est indiquée pour chacune d'elles, ainsi que le nom du concepteur et son adresse électronique, si ces informations sont disponibles.

À l'intérieur de la couverture arrière du livre, vous trouverez un CD-ROM contenant toutes les pages, disposées selon leur emplacement dans l'ouvrage. Vous pouvez les visualiser sur votre moniteur en un temps de chargement minimal et accéder à Internet (sous réserve que vous disposiez d'une connexion) afin d'explorer le site sélectionné dans son intégralité. Le CD contient en outre un dossier au format Macintosh et Windows. Les utilisateurs Mac peuvent naviguer directement à partir du numéro de page correspondant, tandis que sous Windows chaque site se trouve dans un dossier constitué de plusieurs fichiers. Recherchez le fichier «index», «start» ou «default» pour accéder à l'élément de votre choix. En cas de problème, tapez l'adresse URL dans votre navigateur Internet.

Les captures d'écran de l'index et du CD ont été réalisées à l'aide des versions Macintosh d'Explorer 4.5 et de Netscape 4.6, qui autorisent la typographie standard Java et Shockwave. Ces capacités sont intégrées aux navigateurs modernes et peuvent être téléchargées d'Internet gratuitement.

Qualité, innovation et efficacité sont les principaux critères que nous avons utilisés pour sélectionner les sites répertoriés dans cet index. Les sites peuvent se décliner sous toutes les formes, depuis les plus sommaires dotés d'une seule page et de simples éléments de texte, jusqu'aux plus compliqués et percutants intégrant les technologies les plus récentes. Ces deux styles servent un but précis, et tous deux peuvent conjuguer effet visuel et efficacité. C'est pourquoi nous avons intégré ces deux extrêmes dans le livre, ainsi que tous les styles intermédiaires. L'index portant principalement sur la conception de sites, nous n'avons pas cherché à classifier les éléments sélectionnés autrement qu'en regroupant les modèles en fonction de la couleur dominante.

Internet étant un support en évolution constante, des pages conçues il y a seulement un an ou deux peuvent déjà paraître dépassées. De même, il se peut que certaines pages aient subi des modifications ou aient même disparu du réseau depuis que nous les avons sélectionnées pour l'index. Ce dernier offre néanmoins une vue d'ensemble aussi exacte que possible des toutes dernières nouveautés en matière de conception de sites Web.

Tous nos remerciements aux entités ci-dessous pour l'aide qu'elles nous ont apportée dans l'élaboration de cette édition de l'Index de modèles de sites Web : coolhomepages.com, shift.co.jp, la rubrique de Yahoo sur les concepteurs Web, ainsi que le site *shocked site of the day* chez Macromedia (www.shockwave.com).

Les symboles suivants figurent dans le livre :

Site contenant du son

Site contenant de l'animation/vidéo

Propositions de sites :
L'Index de modèles de sites Web sera publié annuellement. Vous pouvez proposer vos sites afin qu'ils paraissent dans la prochaine édition de cet ouvrage en les envoyant à www.webdesignindex.org.

Les ditions Pepin Press/Agile Rabbit
Les éditions Pepin Press/Agile Rabbit publient un vaste éventail de livres et de CD-ROM comportant du matériel de référence visuelle ainsi que des images prêtes à l'emploi destinées aux concepteurs et aux applications Internet, ainsi que des supports imprimés à haute résolution. Pour en savoir plus, rendez-vous sur www.pepinpress.com

Web Design Index

In dieser ersten Ausgabe des Web Design Index werden 1.002 herausragende Webseiten vorgestellt. Soweit sie uns bekannt waren, haben wir zusätzlich zur URL den Designernamen und eine Kontaktadresse angegeben.

Im hinteren Buchdeckel finden Sie eine CD-ROM, die sämtliche im vorliegenden Buch vorgestellten Seiten in der Reihenfolge ihrer Präsentation enthält. Sie können blitzschnell auf die Seiten zugreifen, sich diese auf Ihrem Monitor anschauen und, wenn Sie einen Internetzugang haben, die gesamte Website eingehend im Internet inspizieren. Die CD enthält einen Macintosh- und einen Windowsordner. Mac-Anwender können direkt über die gewünschte Seitennummer navigieren. Wenn Sie einen Windows-Computer haben, so finden Sie jede Site in einem Ordner mit mehreren Dateien. Mit den Dateien "Index", "Start" oder "Default" können Sie dann auf die Datei Ihrer Wahl zugreifen. Sollten hierbei Probleme auftreten, geben Sie einfach die URL in Ihren Internet-Browser ein.

Die Screenshots im Index und auf der CD wurden mit Explorer 4.5 bzw. Netscape 4.6 für MacIntosh hergestellt; benutzt wurde die Standardtypographie, Java und Javascript waren aktiviert und das aktuelle Shockwave-Plugin installiert. Moderne Browser verfügen über diese Java-Funktionen, und das Plugin kann kostenlos aus dem Internet geladen werden (www. shockwave.com).

Designqualität, Innovation, Handhabbarkeit, Verständlichkeit der Navigation und Gesamtwirkung einer Seite bestimmten die Auswahl für diesen Index. Der Inhalt war in keinem Fall Kriterium. Gutes Design erfüllt oder übertrifft die Erwartung der Zielgruppen. Daher sind einfache Sites mit klaren Textlayouts und wenigen Links genauso vertreten wie hochkomplizierte Siteachitekturen mit kurzfilmartigen Einleitungssequenzen. Die Reihenfolge spiegelt keine Wertung wieder, sortiert wurde nach dem Farbeindruck.

Wie kein anderes Medium unterliegt das Internet einem ständigen Wandel. Aus diesem Grund können Seiten, die erst vor einem oder zwei Jahren gestaltet wurden, heute bereits altmodisch erscheinen. Auch kann es sein, dass nach Fertigstellung des vorliegenden Index manche Seiten geändert worden oder sogar ganz aus dem Internet verschwunden sind. Dennoch sind wir der Überzeugung, dass dieser Index einen recht getreuen Überblick über den Stand der Technik in Sachen Web Design bietet.

Folgenden Websites möchten wir für ihre Anregungen bei der Erstellung dieser Ausgabe des Web Design Index danken: coolhomepages.com, shift.co.jp, yahoo.com (Kategorie Web Designer), www.shockwave.com (*shocked site of the day*).

Für das Buch wurden die folgenden Symbole verwendet:

 Web Site mit Audio

 Web Site mit Animation/Video

Beiträge
Der Web Design Index erscheint jährlich. Wenn Sie einen Vorschlag für die nächste Ausgabe des Web Design Index haben, dann wenden Sie sich einfach an die Redaktion: www.webdesignindex.org.

The Pepin Press/Agile Rabbit Editions
The Pepin Press/Agile Rabbit Editions verlegt eine breite Palette an Büchern und CD-ROMs mit Bildreferenzmaterial und gebrauchsfertigen Bildern für Designer, Internetanwendungen sowie hochauflösende Druckmedien.
Nähere Informationen erhalten Sie unter: www.pepinpress.com

Indice del Disegno Web

Questa prima edizione dell'Indice del Disegno Web presenta 1.002 incredibili pagine web. Per ogni pagina è indicata l'URL e, se noto, il nome del disegnatore e il suo indirizzo di posta elettronica.

In terza di copertina troverete un CD-ROM che contiene tutte le pagine disposte in base alla loro ubicazione nel libro. Potrete visualizzarle sul monitor con un tempo di caricamento minimo, ed accedere al sito su Internet (se disponete di un collegamento) per esplorarlo a fondo. Nel CD troverete una cartella per Macintosh e una per Windows. Gli utenti Mac possono navigare direttamente dal numero della pagina corrispondente. Per gli utenti di Windows, ad ogni sito corrisponde una cartella contenente altri file. Cercate i file "index", "start" o "default" per accedere alla vostra scelta. Qualora sorgessero dei problemi, digitate l'URL direttamente nel vostro browser.

Le istantanee delle schermate che appaiono nel libro e nel CD sono state scattate con le versioni Macintosh di Explorer 4.5 e Netscape 4.6, con tipografia standard, Java e Shockwave abilitati. Queste funzionalità sono comuni nei browser attuali e si possono scaricare da Internet gratuitamente.

I criteri principali su cui si fonda la selezione dei siti presenti nell'indice sono l'innovazione e la qualità del disegno, nonché l'efficacia della pagina. Il disegno di pagine web riguarda sia siti di un'unica pagina e con layout semplici di solo testo, sia siti più elaborati, raffinati e tecnicamente all'avanguardia. Entrambi gli stili rispondono a uno scopo particolare, e possono essere ugualmente belli e validi. Pertanto sono entrambi compresi nell'indice, insieme a tutte le categorie intermedie. Poiché il centro d'interesse di questa pubblicazione è il disegno, non è stato fatto alcun tentativo di classificazione della selezione e i lavori sono stati raggruppati in base al colore principale.

Internet è un mezzo soggetto a continue modifiche e quindi alcune pagine disegnate anche solo uno o due anni fa potrebbero già sembrare antiquate. È anche possibile che dopo essere state selezionate, certe pagine siano state modificate o siano scomparse dalla rete. Tuttavia, l'indice presenta una panoramica il più possibile accurata delle ultime tendenze nel campo del disegno di pagine web.

Ringraziamo per la loro collaborazione alla realizzazione di quest'edizione dell'Indice del Disegno Web: coolhomepages.com, shift.co.jp, la sezione di yahoo sui web designer e il sito *shocked site of the day* di Macromedia (www.shockwave.com).

Nel libro sono presenti i seguenti simboli:

   il sito contiene effetti audio

   il sito contiene effetti video/animazione

Presentazione di proposte:

L'Indice del Disegno Web verrà pubblicato annualmente. Le proposte di siti da includere nella prossima edizione devono essere sottoposte a www.webdesignindex.org.

Pepin Press/Agile Rabbit Editions

Le edizioni Pepin Press/Agile Rabbit pubblicano una vasta gamma di libri e CD-ROM con materiale visivo di consultazione e immagini disponibili per disegnatori, applicazioni internet e media ad alta risoluzione di stampa. Per maggiori informazioni visitate il sito www.pepinpress.com.

Índice de diseño de páginas web

Esta primera edición del Índice de diseño de páginas web recoge 1.002 páginas web excelentes. Cada una de ellas incluye su correspondiente dirección URL y, en los casos en los que ha sido posible, el nombre del diseñador o diseñadora y su dirección de correo electrónico.

En la solapa de la cubierta posterior encontrará un CD-ROM que contiene todas las páginas web clasificadas según el lugar que ocupan en este libro. Podrá visualizarlas en el monitor del ordenador tras un tiempo de descarga mínimo y acceder a Internet (siempre y cuando disponga de una conexión) para explorar a fondo la página elegida. En el CD encontrará una carpeta Macintosh y otra Windows. Los usuarios de Macintosh pueden navegar directamente desde el número de página correspondiente. Los usuarios de Windows encontrarán cada una de las páginas web en una carpeta que contiene varios ficheros y deberán buscar el fichero "index", "start" o "default" para acceder a su selección. Si tiene algún problema de acceso, teclee la dirección URL correspondiente en el navegador de Internet.

Las fotografías de las pantallas que aparecen en el libro y en el CD corresponden a las versiones de Explorer 4.5 y Netscape 4.6 para Macintosh, utilizando la tipografía estándar, Java y Shockwave. Las últimas versiones de los navegadores web incorporan todas estas prestaciones, y pueden descargarse de forma gratuita en Internet.

El criterio principal utilizado en esta selección se basa en la calidad y la innovación en relación con el diseño, así como en la efectividad de la página. El diseño de páginas web abarca desde servidores que cuentan con una sola página realizada con un diseño sencillo sólo de texto, hasta estructuras sofisticadas que emplean las prestaciones más innovadoras. Ambas opciones persiguen una determinada finalidad y, tanto una como la otra, pueden resultar atractivas y funcionales. Por tanto, este índice tiene en cuenta los dos tipos de diseño indicados y todos los estilos situados a medio camino entre ambos. El índice se ha confeccionado en base al diseño, por lo que el único tipo de clasificación realizado ha sido ordenar y agrupar los diseños por colores.

Debido a la gran variabilidad de Internet, las páginas diseñadas apenas uno o dos años atrás hoy pueden resultar obsoletas. Asimismo, es posible que algunas páginas se hayan modificado, o incluso hayan desaparecido de la red, desde el momento en que realizamos la selección. No obstante, este índice tiene como objetivo ofrecer una perspectiva lo más precisa posible de las innovaciones en el diseño de páginas web.

Queremos dar las gracias a las entidades que han colaborado en la recopilación del Índice de diseño de páginas web: coolhomepages.com, shift.co.jp, la sección dedicada a los diseñadores de páginas web de yahoo y la sección de la mejor página web del día de Macromedia (*shocked site of the day*; www.shockwave.com).

En este libro se han utilizado los símbolos siguientes:

 página web con sonido

 página web con animación/vídeo

Ediciones:

El Índice de diseño de páginas web se editará anualmente. Si desea que tengamos en cuenta sus diseños para la próxima edición de esta publicación, envíelos a la dirección www.webdesignindex.org.

Pepin Press/Agile Rabbit

La editorial Pepin Press/Agile Rabbit edita una amplia variedad de libros y discos CD-ROM con material de referencia visual e imágenes listas para utilizar de interés para diseñadores, aplicaciones de Internet y medios impresos que trabajan con métodos de alta resolución. Si desea obtener más información al respecto, visite la dirección www.pepinpress.com.

ウェブ・デザイン・インデックス

この初版『ウェブ・デザイン・インデックス』では、1,002の優れたウェブページを紹介します。各ページにはURLのほか、デザイナーの氏名とEメール・アドレスが分かっている場合はこれらも併せて記載されています。

裏表紙内側に収められているCD-ROMには全ページが含まれており、これらは本書掲載ページに従って配置されています。最小のローディング時間でこれらのウェブページをモニターでご覧いただけるほか、（インターネットに接続されている場合は）インターネットにアクセスして、選択されたウェブサイトをすべてご覧いただくことができます。CDにはマッキントッシュとウィンドウズのフォルダがあります。マッキントッシュをご使用の場合は、対応するページ番号から直接ナビゲートできます。ウィンドウズの場合、各サイトはいくつかのファイルからなるフォルダにあります。希望のものにアクセスするには、「インデックス」、「スタート」、あるいは「デフォルト」ファイルを見つけてください。これでうまくいかない場合は、インターネット・ブラウザでURLを入力してください。

インデックスとCD中の写真はマッキントッシュ版のエクスプローラ4.5とネットスケープ4.6を使って撮ったもので、標準タイポグラフィー、Java、Shockwaveを使用しています。これらの機能は最新のブラウザに組み込まれており、インターネットから無料でダウンロードできます。

収録ページの選考には、デザインのクオリティとイノベーション、そしてページ効果が主な基準となっています。ウェブ・デザインは、文章だけを配したシンプルな1ページのホームページから、最新の機能を特徴とする洒落たデザインの複雑な構造のものに至るまで様々です。どちらにも特定の目的があるとともに、どちらも美しくて効果的でありえます。そこで、このインデックスでは、その両方とそれらの中間に位置するあらゆるスタイルのものを取り上げています。ここではデザインに焦点を合わせているため、主たる色に基づいてデザインを配置、グループ分けしているほかには、デザインの分類は行っておりません。

インターネットは先例のない変化を受けやすい媒介であり、ほんの1、2年前に制作されたウェブページがすでに流行遅れに見えることがあります。同様に、私たちがインデックスのためにウェブページを選んだ時点以降に、変更されたページ、あるいはネットから消えているページさえあるかもしれません。それでもなお、このインデックスはできるだけ正確に、最新のウェブ・デザインの概観を伝えているものと思います。

この『ウェブ・デザイン・インデックス』をまとめ上げるにあたりご助力くださったcoolhomepages.com、shift.co.jp、ヤフーのウェブ・デザイナー・セクション、マクロメディアのショックト・サイト・オブ・ザ・デイ（www.shockwave.com）の皆さまに心より感謝申し上げます。

本書では次の記号が使用されています。

音声を含むウェブサイト

動画／画像を含むウェブサイト

デザイン送信：
『ウェブ・デザイン・インデックス』は毎年発行される予定です。次回発行の『ウェブ・デザイン・インデックス』に掲載するデザインの選考を行います。**www.webdesignindex.org** までメールでデザインをご送信ください。

ペピン・プレス／アジャイル・ラビット・エディションズ
ペピン・プレス／アジャイル・ラビット・エディションズは、デザイナー、インターネット・アプリケーションや高解像度印刷媒体用の即使用可能なイメージや視覚的参考データを備える様々な書籍やCD-ROMの発行を手がけています。詳細情報はwww.pepinpress.comをご覧ください。

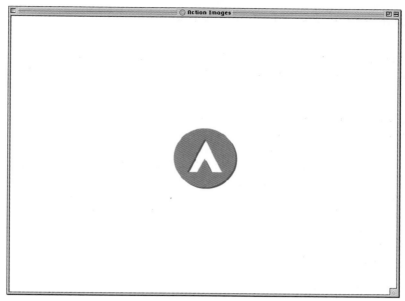

WWW.ACTIONIMAGES.COM/

GERMANY

WWW.ALVR1.COM/DESIGN/PAGES/INTR
JOSEPH LEE ALVIAR | ALVR1 | INFO@ALVR1.COM

WWW.ALVR1.COM/
JOSEPH LEE ALVIAR | ALVR1 | INFO@ALVR1.COM

WWW.SMILEMANAGEMENT.COM/
JAY PRYNNE | TONIC DESIGN LIMITED | WWW.TONICDESIGN.CO.UK   UK

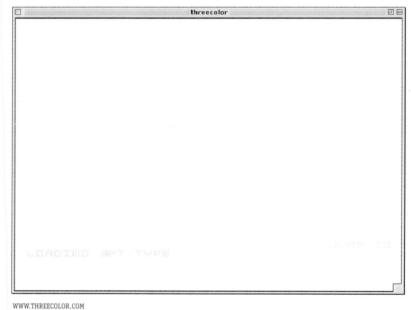

WWW.THREECOLOR.COM
SPENCER | SPENCER@THREECOLOR.COM

WWW.NEOSTREAM.COM/MAIN.HTM
NEOSTREAM INTERACTIVE | WWW.NEOSTREAM.COM

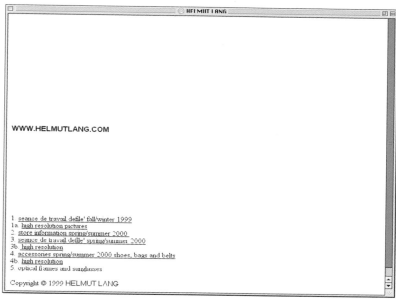

WWW.HELMUTLANG.COM

1. seance de travail defile' fall/winter 1999
1a. high resolution pictures
2. store information spring/summer 2000
3. seance de travail defile' spring/summer 2000
3b. high resolution
4. accessories spring/summer 2000 shoes, bags and belts
4b. high resolution
5. optical frames and sundlasses

Copyright © 1999 HELMUT LANG

WWW.HELMUTLANG.COM/

USA

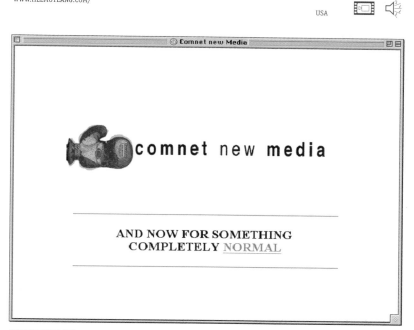

WWW.COMNET.CO.UK/

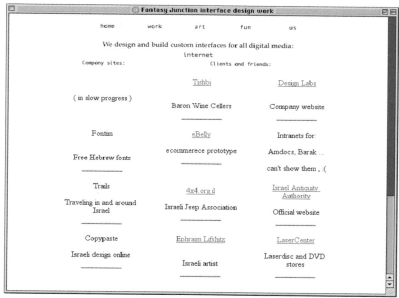

WWW.FANTASY.CO.IL/WORK.HTM
WWW.FANTASY.CO.IL

ISRAEL

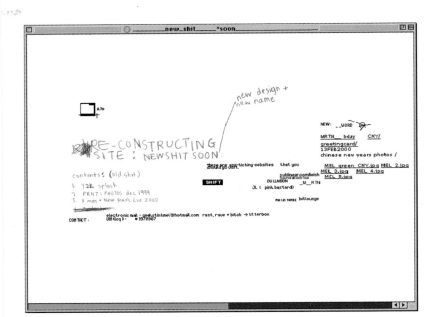

WWW.E-MY.NET.MY/SELANGOR/MELISSACHAN/
MELISSA CHAN | ARTFUDGE@RSUB.COM   MALAYSIA

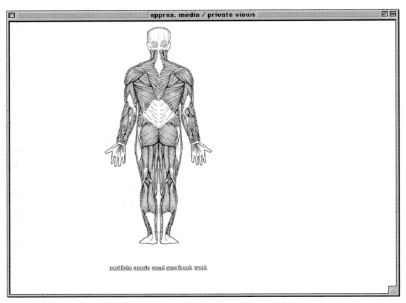

WWW.APPROX.CH/PRIVAT/INDEX.HTML
MICHAEL BÄHNI | DESIGN@APPROX.CH   SWITZERLAND

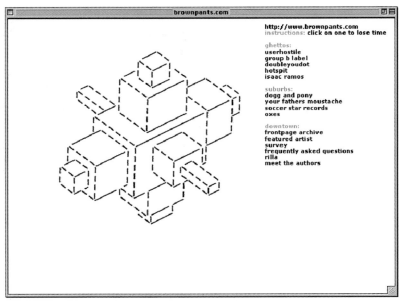

WWW.BROWNPANTS.COM/INDEX.HTM

WWW2.GOL.COM/USERS/SOKADA/
OAKDA SHIGERU

JAPAN

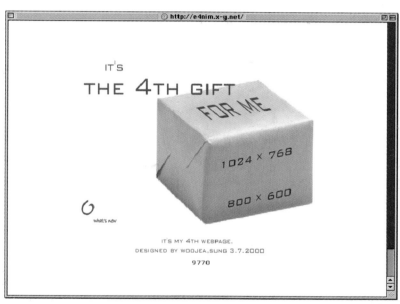

E4NIM.DESIGNKOREA.NET/
SUNG WOOJEA | YHATA@UNITEL.CO.KR

KOREA

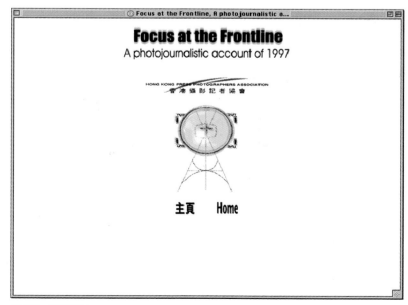

WWW.DG21.COM/HKPPA/
DIGITALONE LTD. | WWW.DG21.COM

HONG KONG

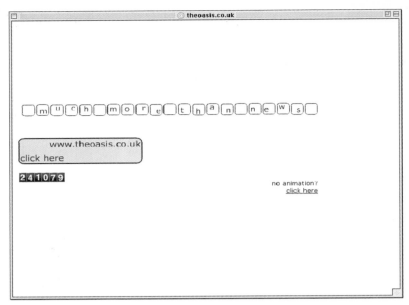

WWW.THEOASIS.CO.UK/
RICHARD GLOVER | RICHARD@THEOASIS.CO.UK UK

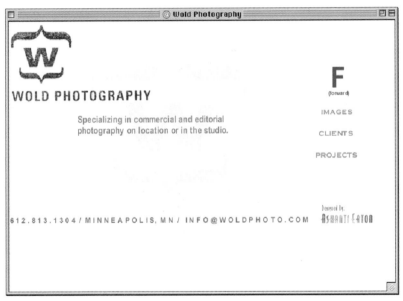

WWW.WOLDPHOTO.COM/MAIN/FRAMES.HTM
MARTIN EATON | ASHANTI EATON | WWW.ASHANTIEATON.COM USA

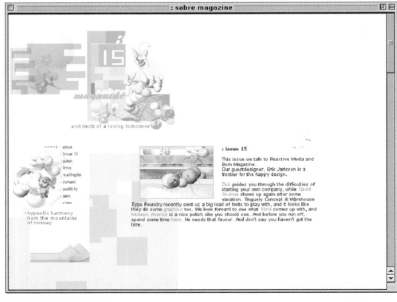

WWW.TRICOM.NO/SABRE/S.HTML

NORWAY

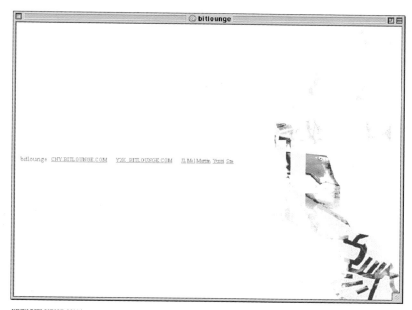

WWW.BITLOUNGE.COM/
JOSH LIM | JL@BITLOUNGE.COM

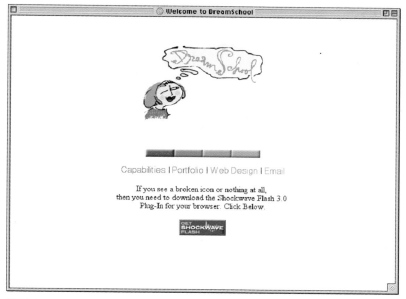

WWW.DREAMSCHOOL.NET/
DREAMSCHOOL INTERACTIVE

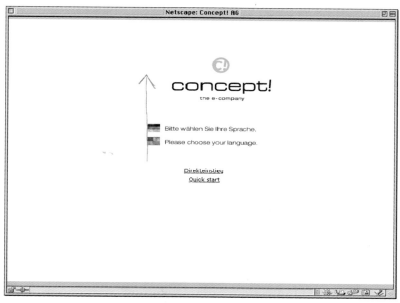

WWW.CONCEPT.COM/
CONCEPT! AG   GERMANY

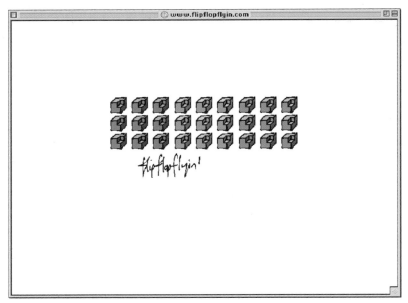

WWW.FLIPFLOPFLYIN.COM
CRAIG ROBINSON | CRAIG@FLIPFLOPFLYIN.COM

WWW.WALKSICILY.DE/
DORIS AMANN, PETER AMANN   ITALY

WWW.SSS.TO/HOME.HTML
SHINJI HAGIUDA   JAPAN

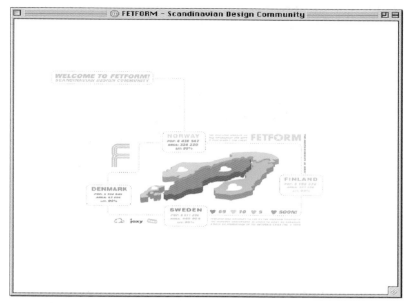

WWW.FETFORM.NET
DICK HANSEN

SWEDEN

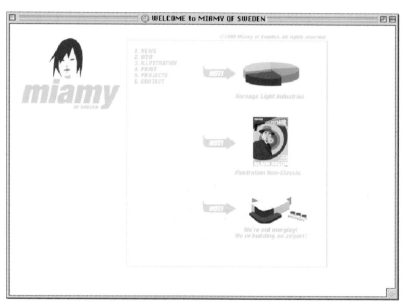

WWW.MIAMY.COM
DICK HANSEN, PATRIK WESTERDAHL

SWEDEN

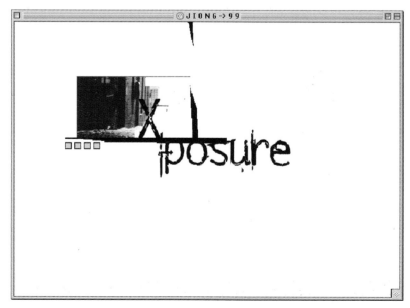

WWW.JIONG.COM/
JIONG LI | JIONG@JIONG.COM

USA

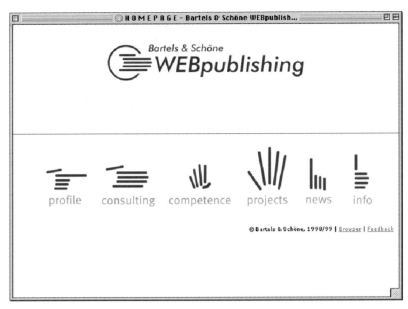

WWW.WEBPUBLISHING.DE/

GERMANY

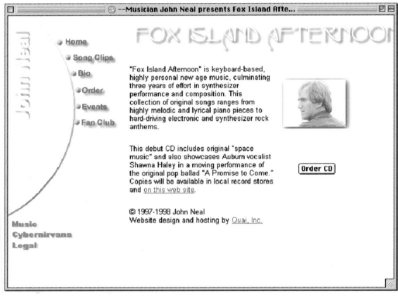

WWW.CYBERNIRVANA.COM/JNEAL/
QUAI, INC | MAIL@QUAI.COM

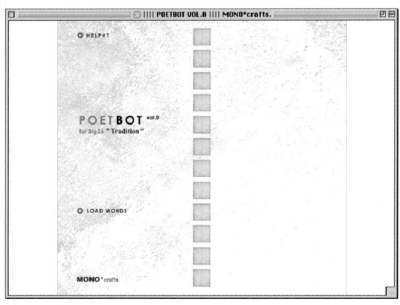

WWW.YUGOP.COM/BIG/BOT.HTML

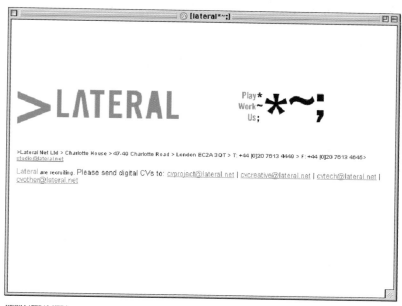

WWW.LATERAL.NET/
ßßßSIMON CRAB, DAVID JONES, SAM COLLET, SIARON HUGHES | LATERAL NET LTD.　　　UK　

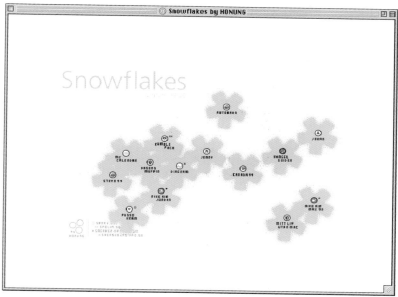

WWW.HONUNG.SE/
JOHAN WISTRAND | JOHAN.WISTRAND@HONUNG.SE　　　SWEDEN　

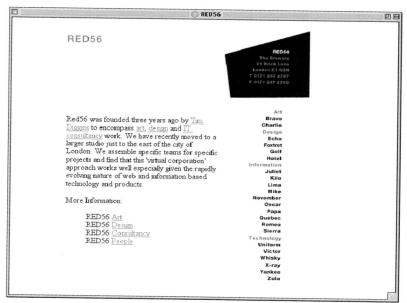

WWW.RED56.CO.UK/
TIM DIGGINS | TEAMWORKS | WWW.TEAMWORKS.CO.UK　　　UK

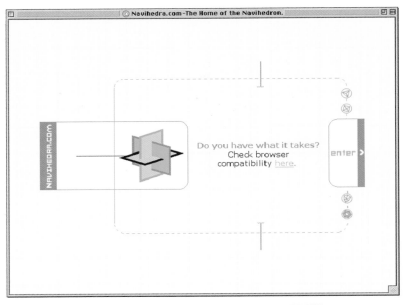

WWW.NAVIHEDRON.COM/

AMAZE LTD | EDITOR@NAVIHEDRA.COM

ADAM TODD, SIMON VAUGHAN, BEN LAST, DANNY BROWN

UK

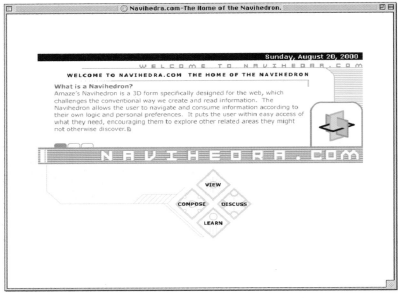

WWW.NAVIHEDRON.COM/AUTH/HOME.HTML

BEN LAST, DANNY BROWN | AMAZE LTD | EDITOR@NAVIHEDRA.COM

ADAM TODD, SIMON VAUGHAN,

UK

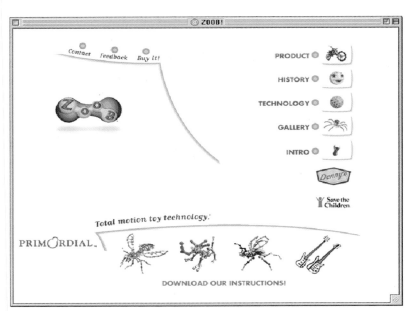

WWW.ZOOB.COM/MAIN.HTML

DUDE@ZOOB.COM, INFO@THUNKDESIGN.COM

MICHAEL JOAQUIN GREY & THUNK DESIGN

USA

WWW.STUDIOMOTIV.COM/COUNTERSPACE/
BRETT YANCY COLLINS, STUDIOMOTIV/MOTIVO | BRETT.COLLINS@MOTIVO.COM   USA

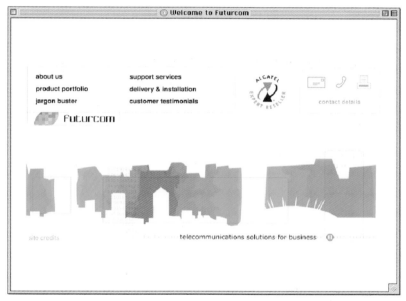

WWW.FUTURCOM.CO.UK/MAIN.HTML
FRONTPAGE | WWW.FRONT-PAGE.CO.UK   UK

WWW.CHURCHILL.CO.UK/
DOMINO SYSTEMS | WWW.DOMINO.COM   UK

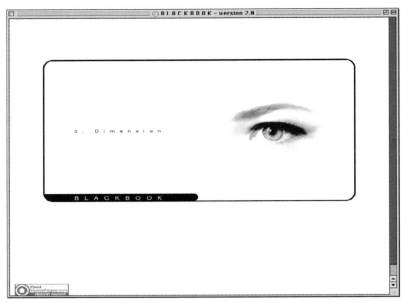

WWW.BLACKBOOK.DK/
JSC@BATES.DK   DENMARK

WWW.HOW.CO.JP/
MASAYUKI NISHIYAMA | STUDIO HOW!? | HOW@HOW.CO.JP   JAPAN

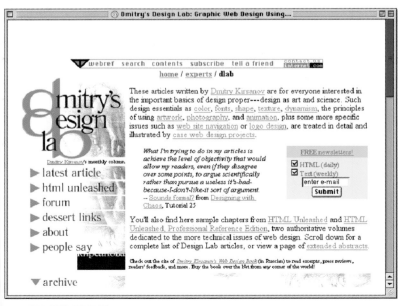

WWW.WEBREFERENCE.COM/DLAB/
DMITRY KIRSANOV | WWW.KIRSANOV.COM

WWW.OSAKAGAS.CO.JP/HTML/LIFE.HTM

JAPAN

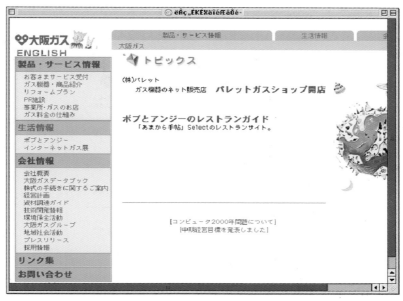

WWW.OSAKAGAS.CO.JP/

JAPAN

WWW.HINTMAG.COM/
HINT FASHION MAGAZINE | HINT@HINTMAG.COM

WWW.I2DESIGN.NET/
ANDY HUMPHRIES | RANDY@I2DESIGN.NET

WWW.MAKS.SE/
KENNETH JACOBSEN | INFO@MAKS.SE   SWEDEN

WWW.VUITTON.COM/VA/HOMA.HTML

                                                   FRANCE

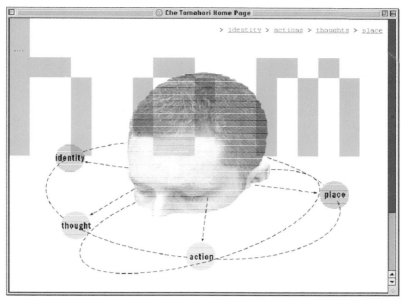

WWW.SFX.CO.NZ/TAMAHORI/HOME
CHE TAMAHORI | CHE@SFX.CO.NZ   NEW ZEALAND

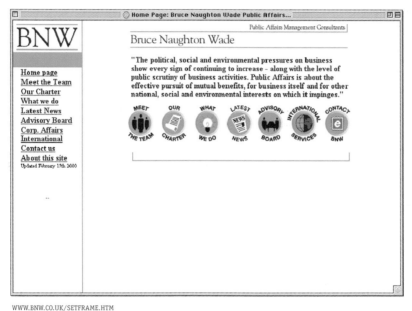

WWW.BNW.CO.UK/SETFRAME.HTM
STEVE WILSON | MOORE-WILSONDESIGN LTD   UK

WWW.ZEPHYR.DTI.NE.JP/~EIEHISA/
IEHISA | IEHISA@ZEPHYR.DTI.NE.JP   JAPAN

WWW.THEWOMEN.NET/
SUNVALLEY COMMUNICATIONS   HONG KONG

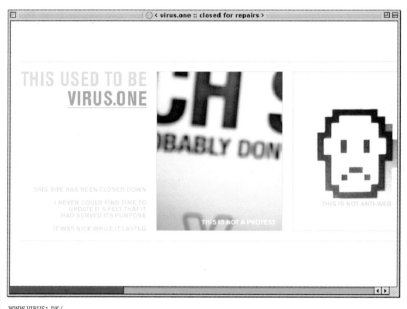

WWW.VIRUS1.DK/
MICHAEL SCHMIDT | VIRUS.ONE | INFO@VIRUS1.DK   DENMARK

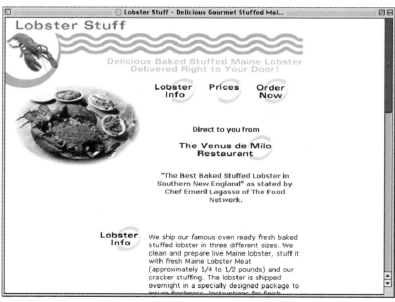

WWW.LOBSTERSTUFF.COM/

                                                           USA

WWW.SEANKERNAN.COM/
SEAN KERNAN, MATTHEW GARRETT   USA

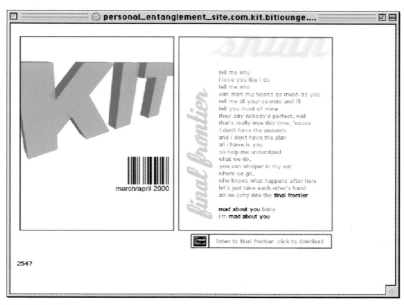

KIT.BITLOUNGE.COM/
                                                                    MALAYSIA

WWW.DEANDELUCA.COM/HTML/INDEX.HTML

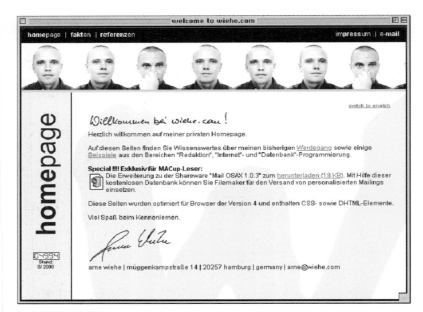

switch to english

homepage

Willkommen bei wiehe.com!

Herzlich willkommen auf meiner privaten Homepage.

Auf diesen Seiten finden Sie Wissenswertes über meinen bisherigen Werdegang sowie einige Beispiele aus den Bereichen "Redaktion", "Internet"- und "Datenbank"-Programmierung.

Special !!!! Exklusiv für MACup-Leser:
Die Erweiterung zu der Shareware "Mail OSAX 1.0.3" zum herunterladen (18 KB). Mit Hilfe dieser kostenlosen Datenbank können Sie Filemaker für den Versand von personalisierten Mailings einsetzen.

Diese Seiten wurden optimiert für Browser der Version 4 und enthalten CSS- sowie DHTML-Elemente.

Viel Spaß beim Kennenlernen.

04994
Stand:
8/2000

arne wiehe | müggenkampstraße 14 | 20257 hamburg | germany | arne@wiehe.com

WIEHE.COM/INDEX_DE.HTML
ARNE WIEHE | WIEHE.COM   GERMANY

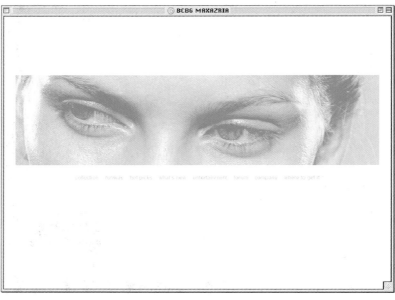

WWW.BCBG.COM/
NORA CHAO, GEORGE WONG | BCBG MAX AZRIA

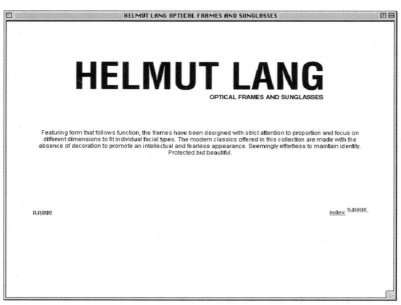

HELMUT LANG
OPTICAL FRAMES AND SUNGLASSES

Featuring form that follows function, the frames have been designed with strict attention to proportion and focus on different dimensions to fit individual facial types. The modern classics offered in this collection are made with the absence of decoration to promote an intellectual and fearless appearance. Seemingly effortless to maintain identity. Protected but beautiful.

p.page   index n.page

WWW.HELMUTLANG.COM/GLASSES/INDEX.HTML
                                                  USA

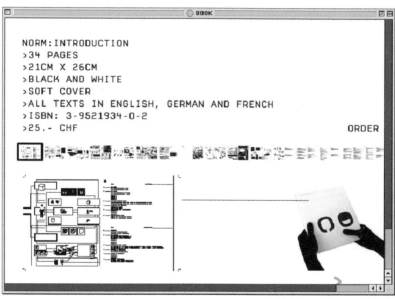

WWW.OKVERSAND.COM
ANDREA KRAUSE, ULRICH RICHTER | WWW.OKVERSAND.COM   GERMANY

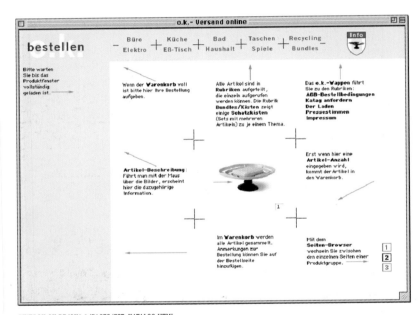

WWW.OK-OK.DE/OK2.3/PAGES/FST_KATALOG.HTML
ANDREA KRAUSE, ULRICH RICHTER | WWW.OKVERSAND.COM   GERMANY

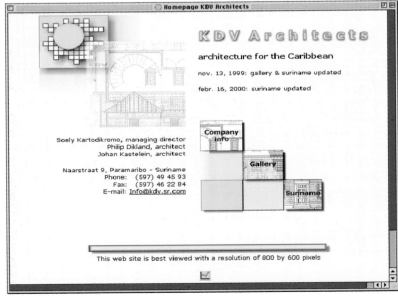

WWW.KDV.SR.COM/
WEB CREATORS | POSTMASTER@WEBCREATORS.SR

WWW.DICKIES.COM/WEB/
JASON PRIOR, GEOFF GROVER, JOHN STURGILL | DICKIESWEB@DICKIES.COM   USA

WWW.FRONTLINE-NET.DE/
WEBMASTER@FRONTLINE-NET.DE   GERMANY

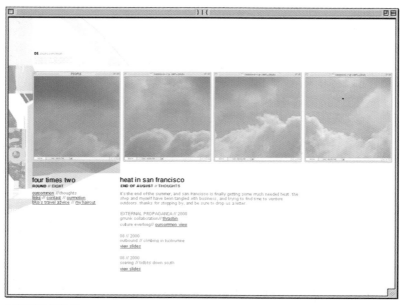

WWW.OURCOMMON.COM
PETER B. REID | PETER@OURCOMMON.COM

WWW.SADLERS-WELLS.COM/
JOE NAVIN | WINONA-DOT.COM | WWW.WINONA-DOT.COM

UK

WWW.FREELOOP.COM/
JEAN-PAUL JACQUET & ZANE GOOD AT SPRINTOUT INTERNET SERVICES

WWW.LUFTHANSA-TECHNIK.DE/E/COMMUNITY/INDEX.HTML
KABEL NEW MEDIA | WWW.KABEL.DE

GERMANY

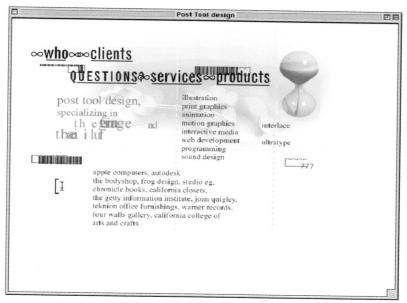

WWW.POSTTOOL.COM/
DAVID KARAM | WWW.POSTTOOL.COM

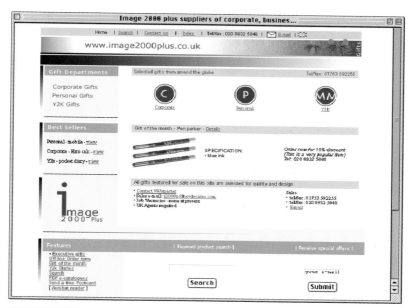

WWW.IMAGE2000PLUS.COM
BAYDESIGNS | INFO@BAYDESIGNS.COM   UK

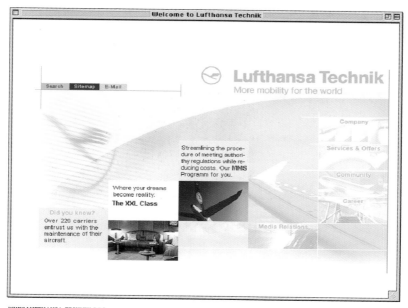

WWW.LUFTHANSA-TECHNIK.DE/
KABEL NEW MEDIA | WWW.KABEL.DE   GERMANY

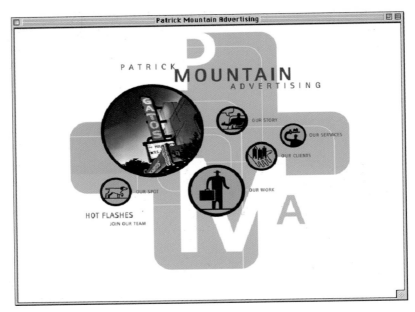

WWW.MOUNTAINADV.COM
KEVIN HERMAN | PATRICK MOUNTAIN ADVERTISING | KEVIN@MOUNTAINADV.COM

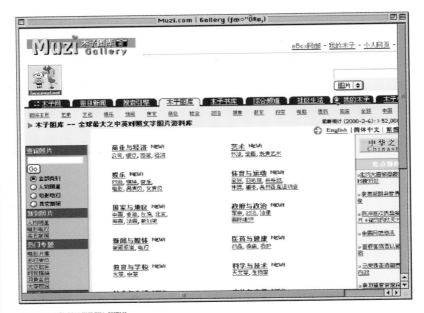

GALLERY.MUZI.COM/INDEX2.SHTML
FRANK LI | MUZI.COM | SUPPORT@MUZI.NET   CHINA

WWW.ASIANNAMES.COM/
WEBSOLUTIONS | WWW.WEBSOLUTIONS.COM.HK   HONG KONG

WWW.INVERTEBRAE.COM/
RYAN HOLSTEN | RYAN@LIFTINGFACES.COM   USA

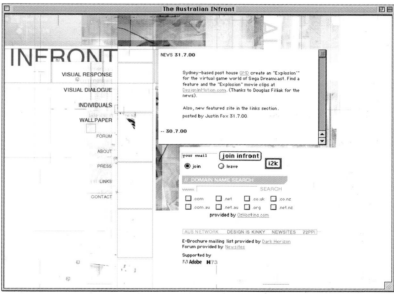

WWW.AUSTRALIANINFRONT.COM.AU
JUSTIN FOX | ANIMAL LOGIC PTY LTD | DFM@DESIGNFIXMEDIA.COM.AU   AUSTRALIA

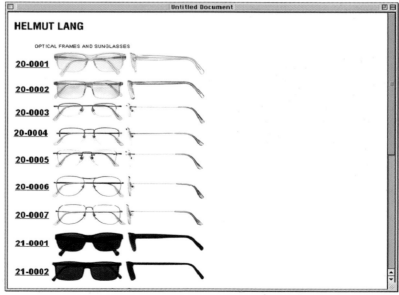

WWW.HELMUTLANG.COM/GLASSES/INDEX2.HTML

USA

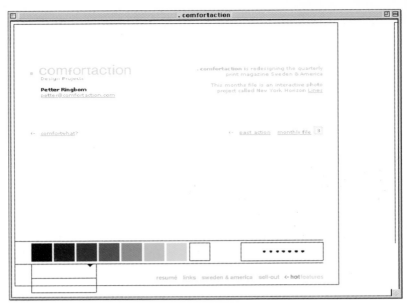

WWW.COMFORTACTION.COM/PORTFOL.HTML
PETTER RINGBOM | PETTER@COMFORTACTION.COM USA

WWW.DEEPZOO.COM/
WILLIAM ETUNDI JR. | WE@DEEPZOO.COM USA

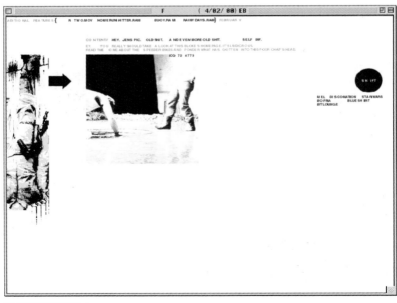

MS.BITLOUNGE.COM/FEB_/
MARTIN SMEDSÉN | NILSPETR@HEM1.PASSAGEN.SE SWEDEN

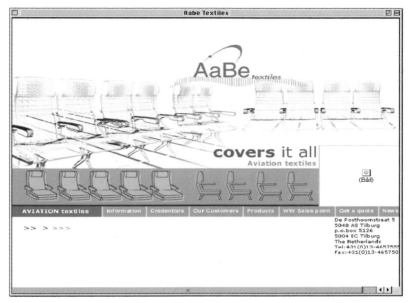

WWW.AABE.NL/

WWW.NITROUSA.COM/HOME_FRAMESET.HTML
OLAF CZESCHNER | NEUE DIGITALE | WWW.NEUE-DIGITALE.DE

GERMANY

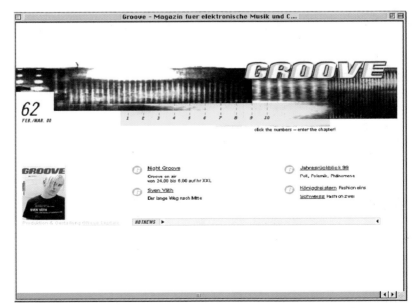

WWW.GROOVE.DE/HOME.HTM
NEUE DIGITALE | WWW.NEUE-DIGITALE.DE

GERMANY

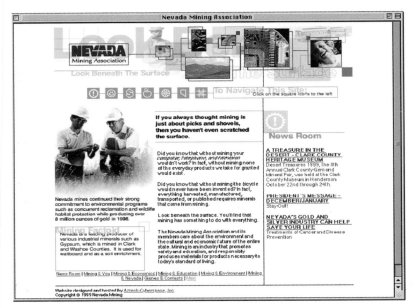

WWW.NEVADAMINING.ORG/

USA

WWW.INTENSIVE-CARE-MONITOR.COM/
DEEP CREATIVE LTD. | WWW.DEEP.CO.UK

UK

WWW.SAWYERANDFINN.COM/

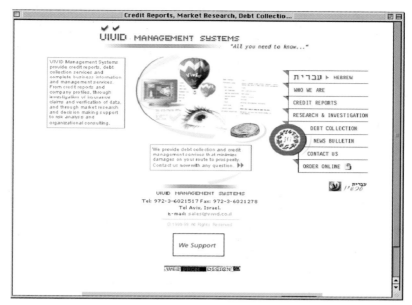

WWW.VIVID.CO.IL/
WEBPROM DESIGN | WWW.WEB-DESIGN.CO.IL   ISRAEL

WWW.SOVA.RU/ARTCATALOG/AWARD

RUSSIA

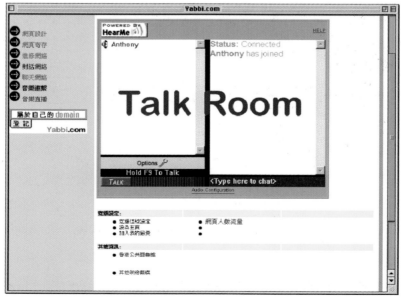

WWW.YABBI.COM
INFO@YABBI.COM   JAPAN

WWW.THERAINFORESTSITE.COM
DANIEL ACHILLES | PRECINCT° DESIGN LEGION | WWW.PRECINCT.NET   SWEDEN

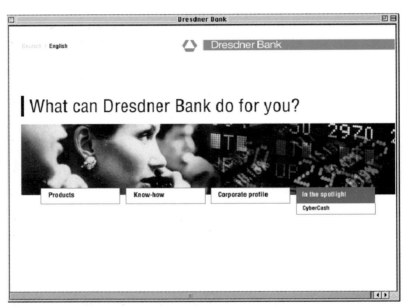

WWW.DRESDNER-BANK.COM/

                                                                GERMANY

WWW.AZUR.FR/HOME/
INFO@AZUR.FR   FRANCE

WWW.DPLUS.DE/
GÜNTHER BOGDAN | WEBMASTER@DPLUS.DE

GERMANY

FAIRAGENCY.CZ/INDEX.HTM
JAKUB DITRICH | GLOBE INTERNET | GLOBE-INTERNET.COM

CZECH REPUBLIC

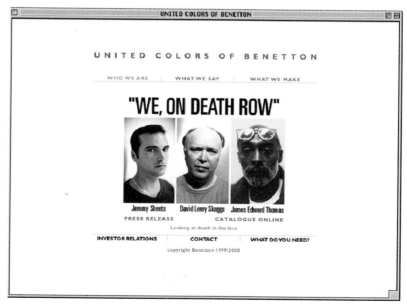

WWW.BENETTON.COM/INDEX.CGI

ITALY

WWW.ANGLESEY.GOV.UK/
WALES INTERNET SERVICES | WISS@WISS.CO.UK UK

WWW.NAUTICA.COM/MAIN_FRAMESET_3.HTML DAN BENDERLY
ZENTROPY PARTNERS & NAUTICA ENTERPRISES | HHELLER@ZENTROPYPARTNERS.COM USA

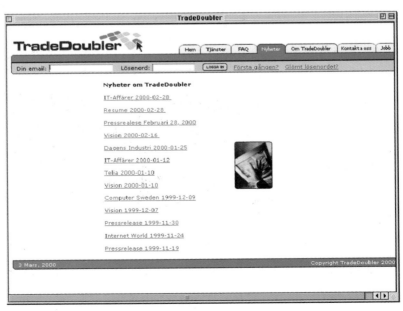

WWW.TRADEDOUBLER.COM/PUBLIC/DEFAULT.ASP?TEXT_KEY=NEWS
WWW.E-TECHFACTORY.COM UK

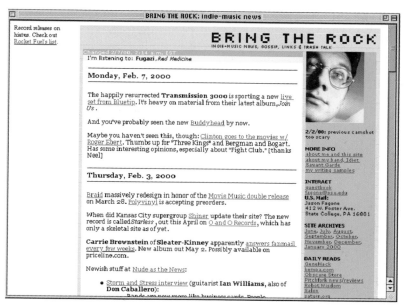

WWW.REIFY.ORG/
JASON FAGONE

WWW.SIXTY.NET/SIXTY.HTM
THESIGN SOLUTIONS STUDIO | WWW.THESIGNSOLUTIONS.COM

RANIERO CITARELLA, TIZIANO SILVESTRI
ITALY

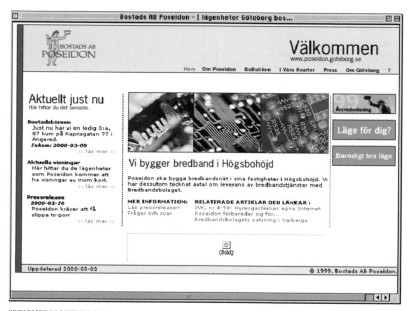

WWW.POSEIDON.GOTEBORG.SE/
KENNETH JACOBSEN | MAKS MEDIA | KENNETH@MAKS.SE

SWEDEN

WWW.INNOFTHEGOVERNORS.COM/
JENNIFER MARTIN | XYNERGY INTERACTIVE | WWW.XYNERGY.COM USA

WWW.LECHTERSONLINE.COM/EXPLORE
KIOKEN INCORPORATED | WWW.KIOKEN.COM USA

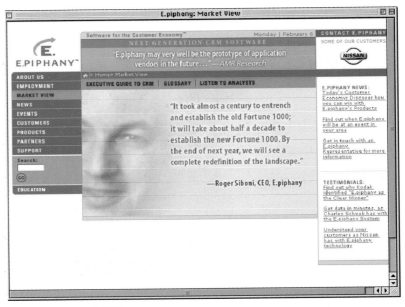

WWW.EPIPHANY.COM/MARKET/INDEX
METRIUS | WWW.METRIUS.COM

WWW.STATICLIFE.COM/SHALLOW
SUN AN | 08@STATICLIFE.COM   USA

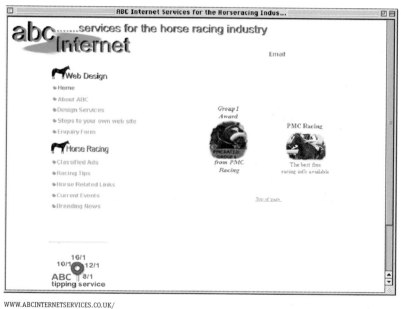

WWW.ABCINTERNETSERVICES.CO.UK/
ABC INTERNET SERVICE   UK

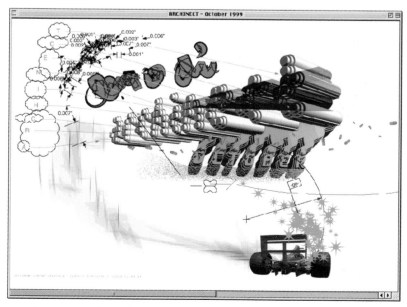

WWW.ARCHINECT.COM/INDEXRARE.HTML
PAUL PETRUNIA, COVER BY CLANCY PEARSON | PAUL@ARCHINECT.COM   USA

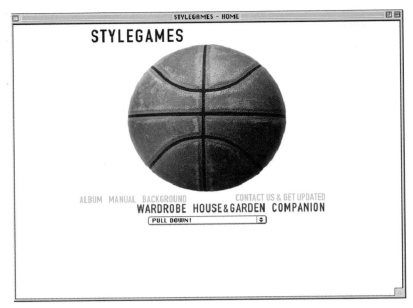

WWW.STYLEGAMES.NET/
HOLGER FRIESE | HOLGER FRIESE KOMMUNKATION | WWW.FUENFNULLZWEI.DE   GERMANY

WWW.STYLEGAMES.NET/ENTERPAGES/PAPER-SKIRT.HTML
HOLGER FRIESE | HOLGER FRIESE KOMMUNKATION | WWW.FUENFNULLZWEI.DE   GERMANY

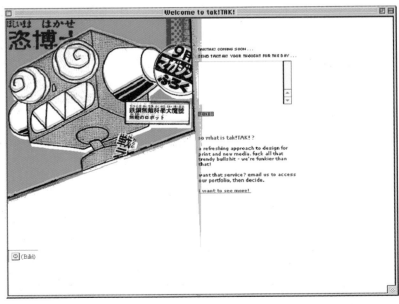

WWW.TAKTAK.CO.UK/
DOM MURPHY | TAK!TAK! | I_WANT_A_TAKTAK@TAKTAK.CO.UK   UK

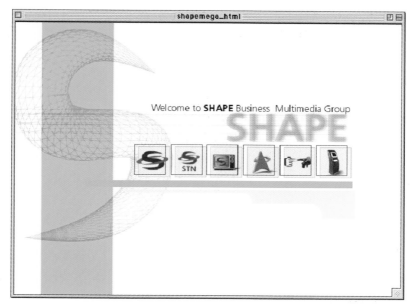

WWW.SHAPE.CO.IL/DEFAULT_HTML.HTML
INFO@SHAPE.CO.IL   ISRAEL

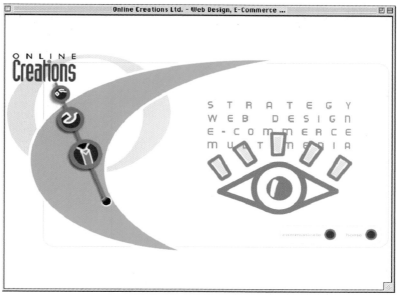

WWW.ONLINE-CREATIONS.COM/

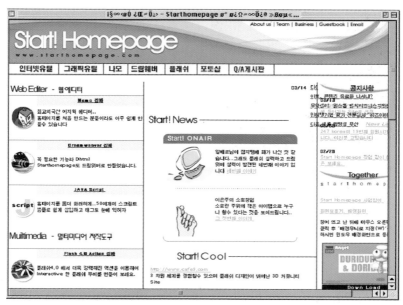

WWW.STARTHOMEPAGE.COM/MAIN.HTM

                                  HONG KONG

POCHI.I-YOUNET.NE.JP/JIN/INDEX-2.HTML

JAPAN

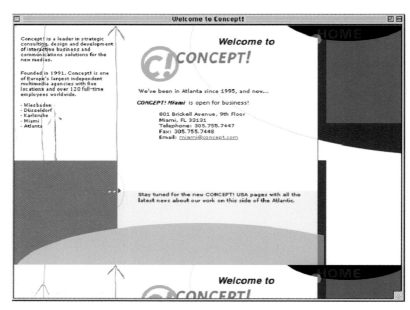

WWW.CONCEPT.COM/INDEX_E.HTML
CONCEPT! AG

GERMANY

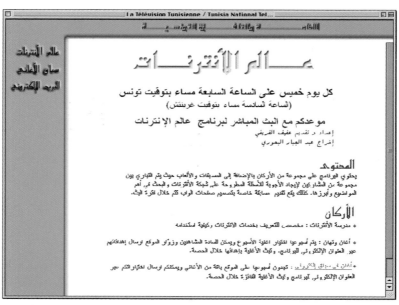

WWW.TUNISIATV.COM/INTERNET/INDEX.HTML

TUNISIA

WEB4.SUPERB.NET/ARIEL/
ARIEL MALKA | ARIEL_ML@NETVISION.NET.IL   ISRAEL

WWW.730CREATIVE.COM/HOME.HTM

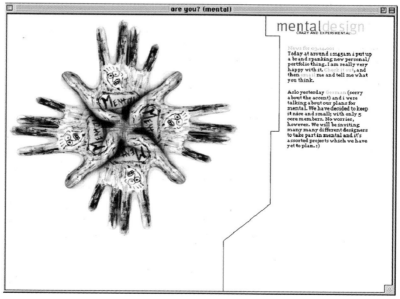

WWW.MENTAL.NU/
ERROL RICHARDSON | ERROL@MENTAL.NU   UK

WWW.DINGRAFIK.COM/WORK/
JASON KRISTOFER | INFO@DINGRAFIK.COM

USA

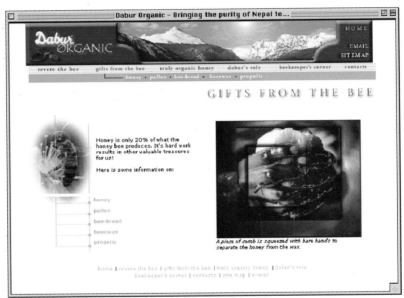

WWW.DABURORGANIC.COM/GIFTSINDEX.HTML
INFO@DABURORGANIC.COM

WWW.CUHK.HK/

HONG KONG

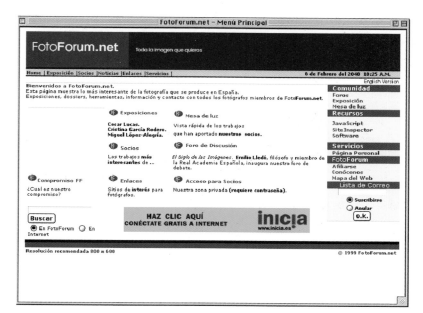

WWW.FOTOFORUM.NET/
FERNANDO MATEUS

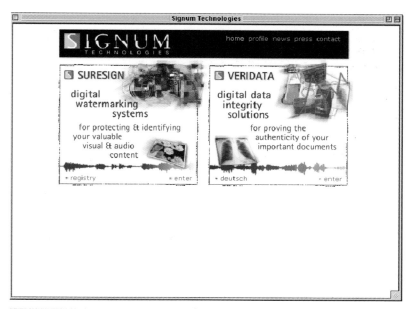

WWW.SIGNUMTECH.COM/
ALANB@SIGNUMTECH.COM   UK

WWW.SYRIA-ONLINE.COM/

SYRIA

WWW.TOPSETHOTEL.COM/
JAUD MARIA | INFO@TOPSETHOTEL.COM   CYPRUS

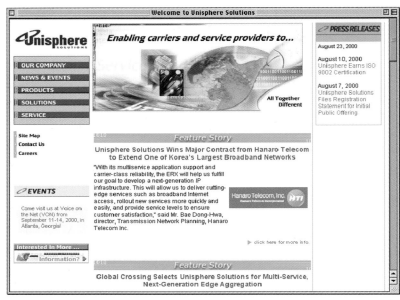

WWW.UNISPHERESOLUTIONS.COM/
                                                USA

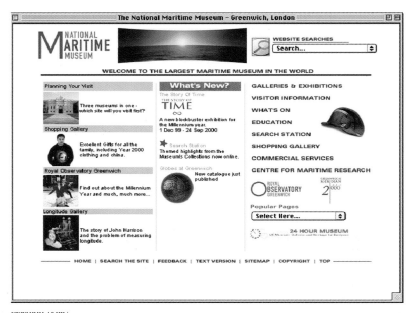

WWW.NMM.AC.UK/
SOPHIA ROBERTSON | NATIONAL MARITIME MUSEUM | NMMWEB@NMM.AC.UK   UK

60

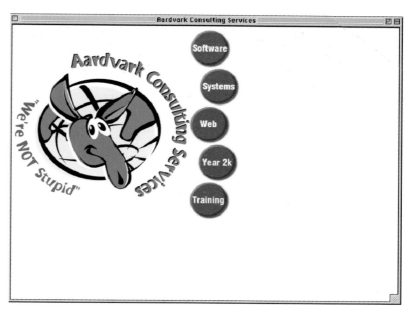

WWW.2AARDVARKS.COM/
JIM LOWE | JLOWE@ADVERTISING.COM

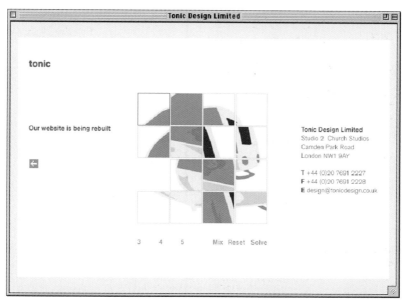

WWW.TONICDESIGN.CO.UK/
TONIC DESIGN

UK

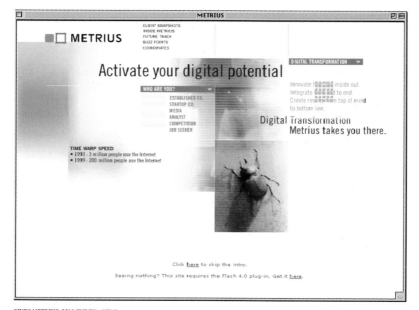

WWW.METRIUS.COM/INDEX2.HTML
METRIUS | WWW.METRIUS.COM

USA

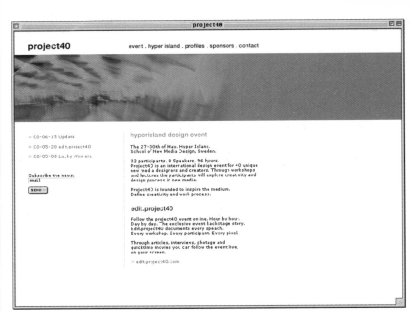

WWW.PROJECT40.COM
HENRIK KARLSSON, MARIA NOHLSTRÖM, LISA LINDSTRÖM | LISA@PROJECT40.COM   SWEDEN

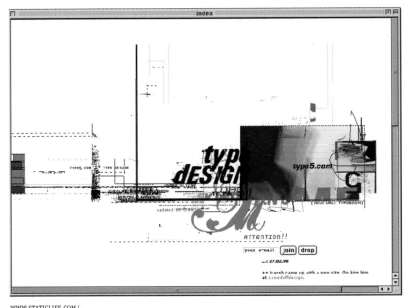

WWW.STATICLIFE.COM/
SUN AN | 08@STATICLIFE.COM   COLOMBIA

WWW.STATICLIFE.COM/
SUN AN | 08@STATICLIFE.COM   USA

WWW.DISCOVERAVENTURA.COM/

USA

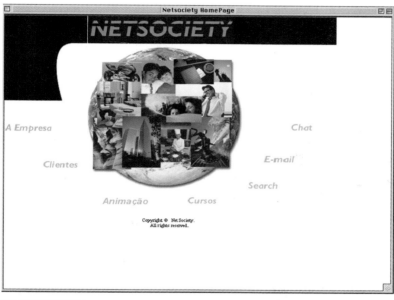

WWW.NETSOCIETY.COM.BR/
EDUARDO FALCÃO | AHI@NETSOCIETY.COM.BR

BRAZIL

WWW.ESSEXCC.GOV.UK/
MARC GARNERS | SIXTYEIGHT CREATIVE SOLUTIONS | SOLUTIONS@SIXTYEIGHT.CO.UK

UK

WWW.SPORTINGLIFE.COM
ALIX WOODING | SPORTINGLIFE.COM | FEEDBACK@SPORTINGLIFE.COM   USA

WWW.STILESGROUP.COM/HOME.HTML
BETH BAST | BETHBAST@BBD.COM   USA

NTUDLM.CSIE.NTU.EDU.TW/DEFAULT.HTML
          TAIWAN

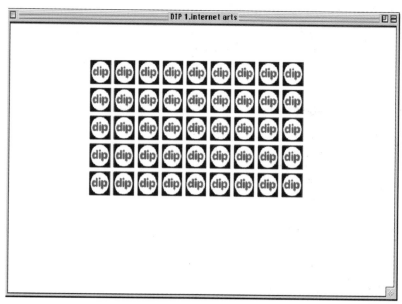

WWW.THECOOKER.COM/HERE/DIP.HTML
JAKE TILSON | ©ATLAS 1994-2000 | JAKE@THECOOKER.COM   USA

WWW.ULOGEAR.COM/
BRIAN SANCHEZ | DEMIGRAPHICS.COM | INFO@ULOGEAR.COM

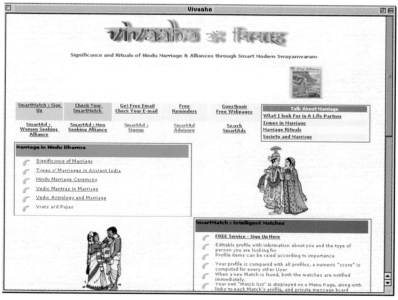

WWW.VIVAAHA.ORG/
GLOBAL HINDU ELECTRONIC NETWORKS | WWW.GHEN.NET   INDIA

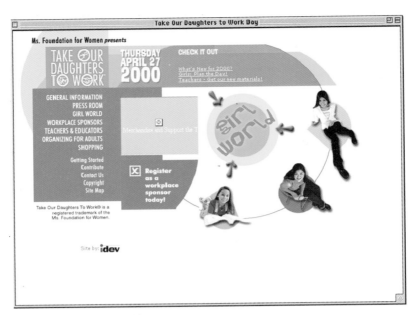

WWW.TAKEOURDAUGHTERSTOWORK.ORG/
IDEV | WWW.IDEV.COM   USA

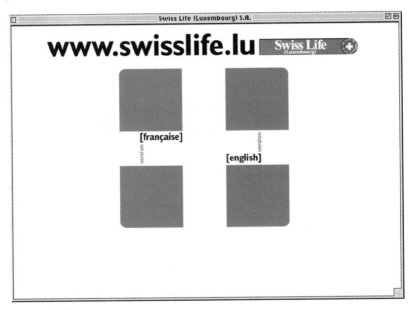

WWW.SWISSLIFE.LU/
RED DOG COMMUNICATIONS S.A. | WWW.RED-DOG.COM   LUXEMBOURG

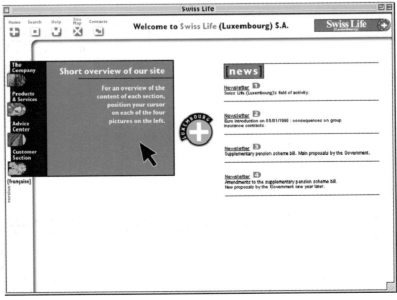

WWW.SWISSLIFE.LU/INDEX_E.HTM
RED DOG COMMUNICATIONS S.A. | WWW.RED-DOG.COM   LUXEMBOURG

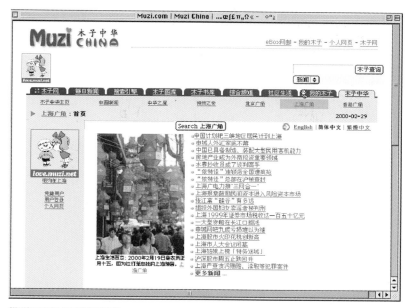

SHANGHAI.MUZI.NET/INDEX2.SHTML
FRANK LI | MUZI.COM

CHINA

WWW.THEWOMEN.NET/BEAUTY/JAN2000/
SUNVALLEY COMMUNICATIONS

HONG KONG

WWW.GRAFIKAS.COM/VERSION1/
DREW EUROPEO | SPEAK@GRAFIKAS.COM

PHILIPPINES

WWW.YOUGLOWGIRL.COM/GLOWHOME.HTM

USA

WWW.BRAINSTORM.CO.ZA/
WILLIAM@BRAINSTORM.CO.ZA

SOUTH AFRICA

WWW.DISTURBED.COM/2.0/
MATT PETTY | MATT@DISTURBED.COM

WWW.JLINDEBERG.COM/   JAKOB SWEDENBORG, JOHAN BRANDSTRÖM , JENNY ROSÉN
SATAMA INTERACTIVE | WWW.SATAMA.COM   SWEDEN

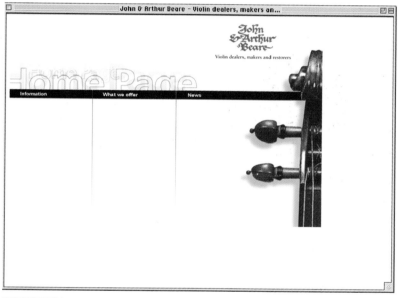

WWW.BEARES.COM/
SELMAN@BEARES.COM

WWW.MANKAS.COM/MANKA'S.HTM
LARRY BARNETT | BARNETT MARKETING | WWW.BARNETTMARKETING.COM   USA

WWW.DIESEL.CO.UK/STORE/HOME_GIF.HTML   RICHARD HOLLEY, TREVOR CHAMBERS
WWW.DIESEL.COM & EHSREALTIME | WWW.EHSREALTIME.COM | WWW.DIESEL.COM   UK

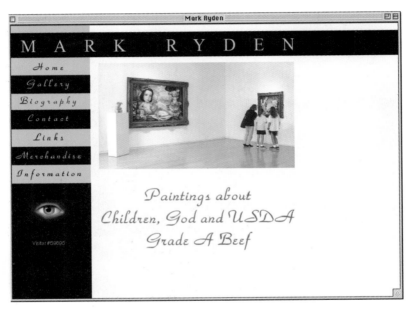

WWW.MARKRYDEN.COM/
KEVIN SPARKS   USA

WWW.COOPERKATZ.COM/
NOAH DAVIS   USA

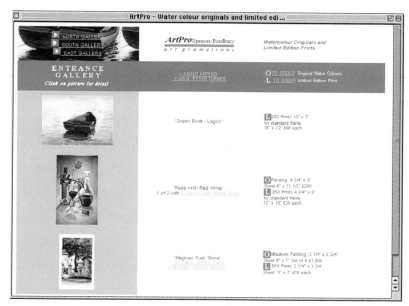

WWW.ARTPRO.CO.UK/
PETER TURNER | ANGLOWEBS | WWW.ANGLOWEBS.COM   UK

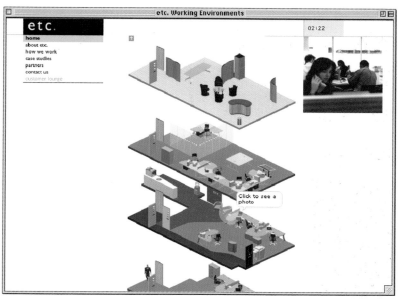

WWW.ETC-UK.COM/HTML
SIMON HEYS | WWW.TONICDESIGN.CO.UK   UK

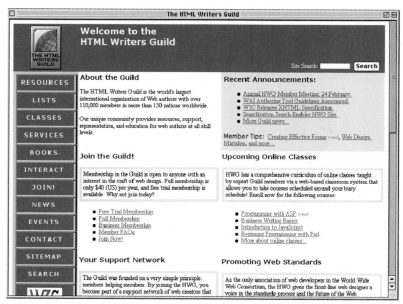

WWW.HWG.ORG/

USA

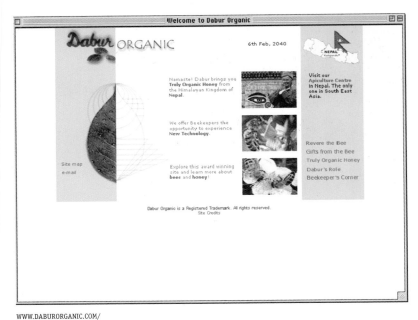

WWW.DABURORGANIC.COM/
NFO@DABURORGANIC.COM

WWW.LOVELLPARTNERSHIPS.CO.UK/
FLG21 | WWW.FLG21.COM   UK

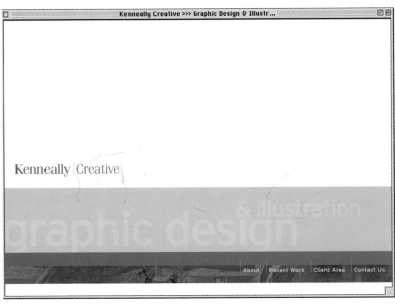

WWW.KENNEALLYCREATIVE.COM
ANDY LIM | ANDY@ARTDIRECTORS.COM   MALAYSIA

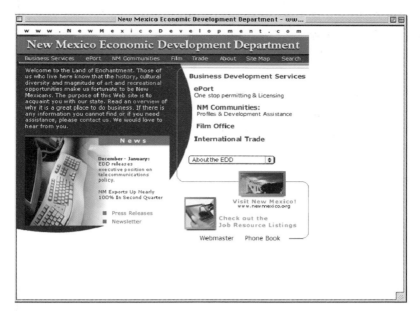

WWW.EDD.STATE.NM.US/
JENNIFER MARTIN | XYNERGY INTERACTIVE | WWW.XYNERGY.COM　　　　　　　　USA

WWW.TOUCHCTS.COM/
MELROSE ANG | BALLYHOO INTERNATIONAL SERVICES | WWW.BALLYNET.COM

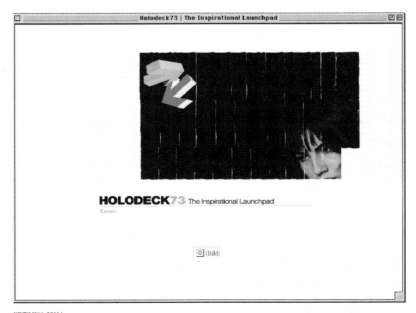

WWW.H73.COM/
M. MEJIA | MAT@DROPPOD.COM

WWW2.GOL.COM/USERS/SOKADA/INDEX2.HTML
OAKDA SHIGERU

JAPAN

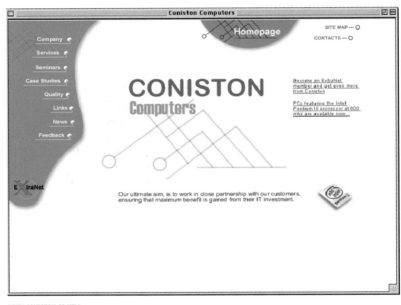

WWW.CONISTON.CO.UK/
KEITH.ROWE@CONISTON.CO.UK

UK

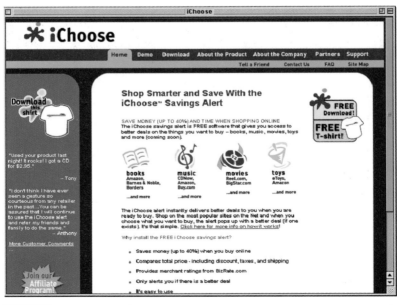

ICHOOSE.COM/
KEVIN LOFGREN | ICHOOSE, INC. | LOFGREN@ICHOOSE.COM

USA

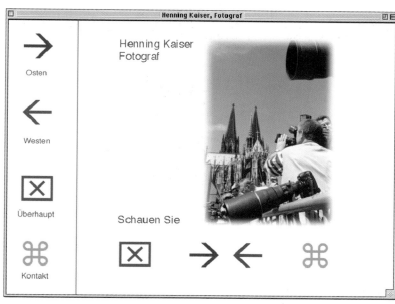

WWW.HENNING-KAISER.DE
HENNING KAISER | KAISER@TRANSPARENT-PHOTO.DE GERMANY

WWW.VISIONS.MEDIATRUST.ORG SIMON CRAB, DAVID JONES, SAM COLLET,
SIARON HUGHES | LATERAL NET LTD. | WWW.LATERAL.NET UK

WWW.BAYDESIGNS.COM/WS/
BAYDESIGNS | INFO@BAYDESIGNS.COM UK

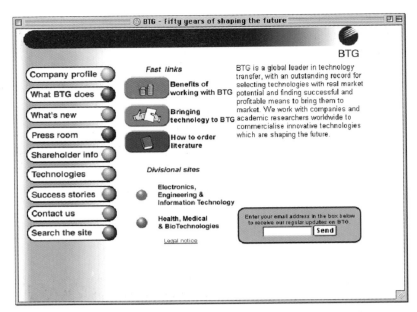

WWW.BTGPLC.COM/
HALESWAY LIMITED   UK

WWW.CORNCOTT.COM
ASH MASHHADI | DESIGN INSPIRATIONS | ASHM@INSPIRATION.CO.UK   UK

WWW.ISARFOTO.DE/HTML/HOME.HTM
WWW.NETAFFAIR.DE   GERMANY

WWW.KINKOS.COM/

WWW.LEARN.COM/
PATRICK TOOMEY | LEARN.COM, INC.

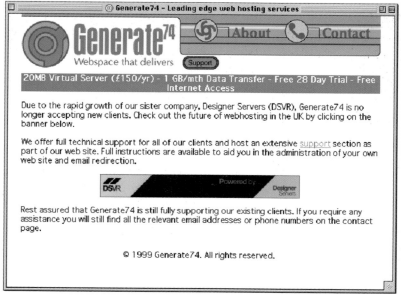

WWW.GENERATE74.CO.UK/

UK

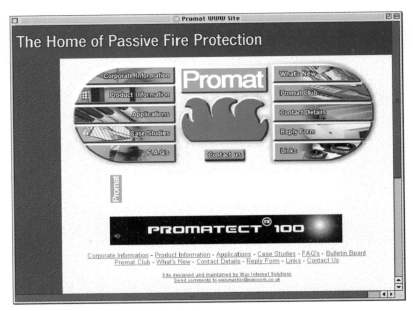

WWW.PROMAT.CO.UK/WEB/INDEX.HTM
ANDY GOODE | WAX DIGITAL | WWW.WAXCOM.CO.UK UK

CHANDRA.HARVARD.EDU/
KIMBERLY L. KOWAL | FUNDING FROM NASA CNAS8-39073 | CXCPUB@CFA.HARVARD.EDU USA

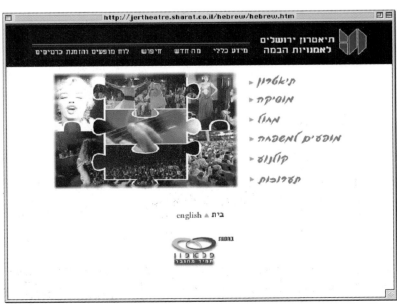

JERTHEATRE.SHARAT.CO.IL/HEBREW/HEBREW.HTML
SHARAT LTD. | SHARAT.CO.IL ISRAEL

WWW.CHECKSINTHEMAIL.COM/
CHECKS IN THE MAIL | MWIER@CARADON.COM

USA

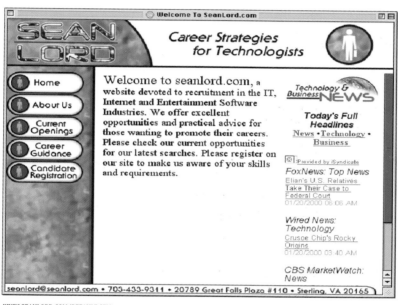

WWW.SEANLORD.COM/DEFAULT.CFM
SEAN LORD | DIGEX

UK

WWW.ENERGIE.IT/ENTER.HTM
THESIGN SOLUTIONS STUDIO | WWW.THESIGNSOLUTIONS.COM

RANIERO CITARELLA, TIZIANO SILVESTRI
ITALY

WWW.PURDEYS.DE/INDEX_P.HTML
PROJECT.INTERNETGROUP | WEBMASTER@PROJECT.DE

MARKUS DEUERLEIN, ROLAND KARGEL
GERMANY

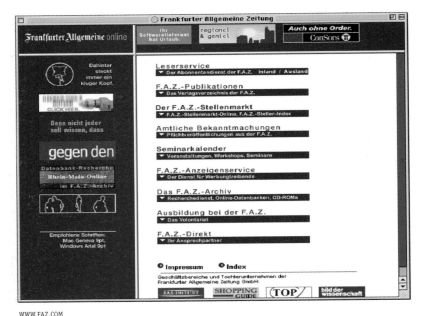

WWW.FAZ.COM
JENS LÖBBE | F.A.Z. ELECTRONIC MEDIA GMBH

GERMANY

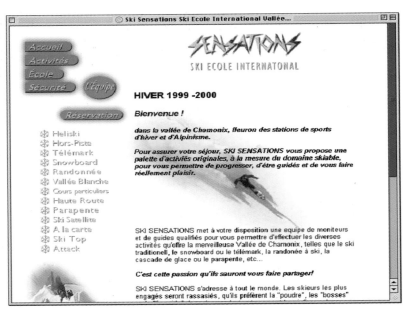

WWW.SKI-SENSATIONS.COM
LARS FORNELL AND NICK BRANDT | LIMELAB WEB DEVELOPMENT | WWW.LIMELAB.COM

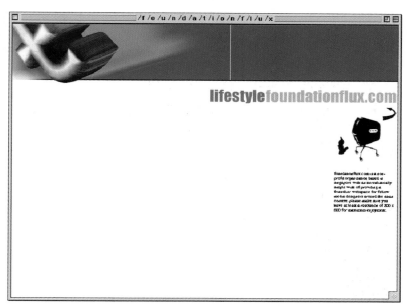

WWW.FOUNDATIONFLUX.COM/
ADRIAN AND JIMMY | ETC/WOOFERXP PRODUCTION © | INPUT@FOUNDATIONFLUX.COM

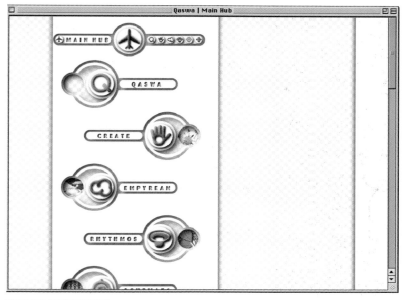

WWW.QASWA.COM/MNMENU.HTML

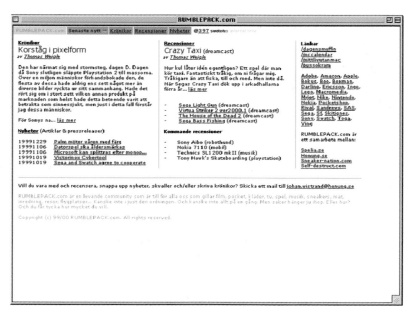

WWW.HONUNG.SE/RUMBLEPACK/
JOHAN WISTRAND | JOHAN.WISTRAND@HONUNG.SE   SWEDEN

WWW.E3DIREKTIV.COM/MAIN.HTML
FUSION MEDIA GROUP | INFO@E3DIREKTIV.COM   CANADA

WWW.NIERI.IT/
NIERI@NIERI.IT   ITALY

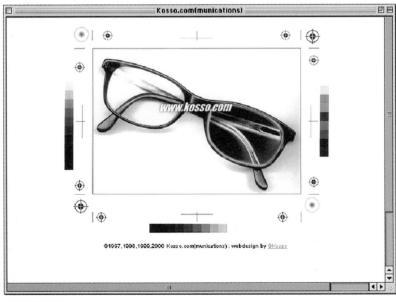

WWW.KOSSO.COM/
JON KOSSMANN | KOSSO@KOSSO.COM   UK

WWW.NINETIES.COM.HK/INDEX-B5.HTM

HONG KONG

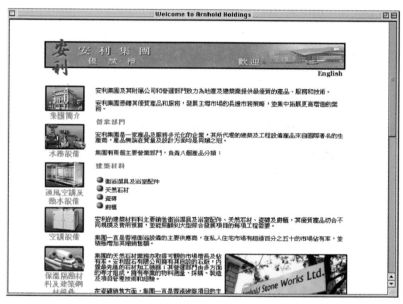

WWW.ARNHOLD.COM.HK/CHINESE/INDEX.HTM

HONG KONG

WWW.CHINAPRO.COM/CGI-BIN/VIEWNEWS.CGI?CATEGORY=2&ID=947844955
CHINAPRO | WWW.CHINAPRO.COM

USA

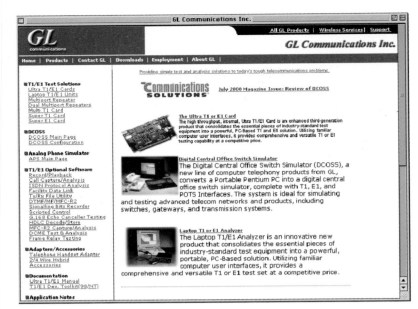

WWW.GL.COM/DEFAULT.HTML

ALAN CHEUNG | WORLD WIDE WEB GLOBAL LTD. | CYBERNETIC.COM.HK HONG KONG

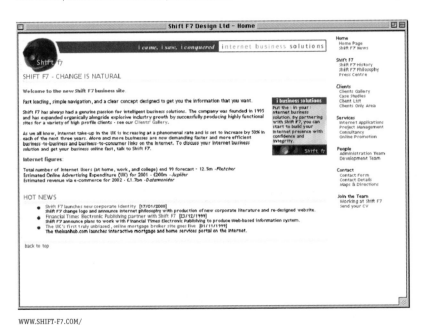

WWW.SHIFT-F7.COM/

SEAN@SHIFT-F7.COM UK

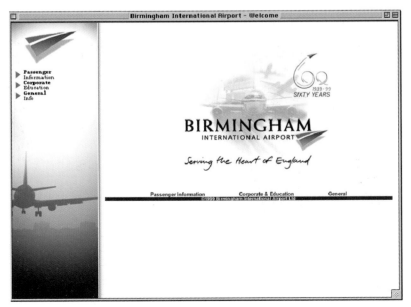

WWW.BHX.CO.UK/

BIRMINGHAM INTERNATIONAL AIRPORT LIMITED UK

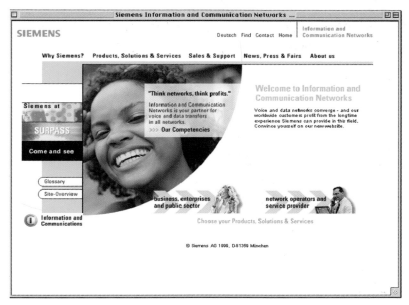

WWW.SIEMENS.DE/IC/NETWORKS/

GERMANY

WWW.ADVANCEDESIGN.DE/
ADVANCE DESIGN

GERMANY

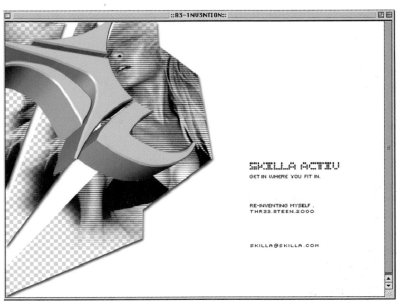

WWW.SKILLA.COM/
BERNARD MAGALE [SKILLA]

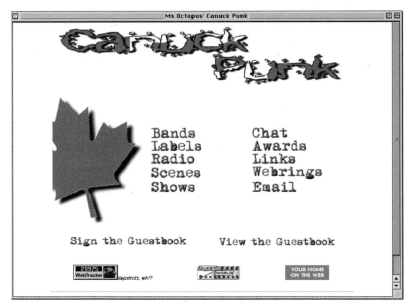

WWW.GEOCITIES.COM/SUNSETSTRIP/ALLEY/8941/
ERIC FLEXYOURHEAD | FLXYRHED@DIRECT.CA   CANADA

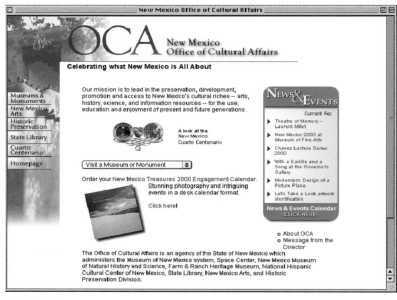

WWW.NMOCA.ORG/
JENNIFER MARTIN | XYNERGY INTERACTIVE | WWW.XYNERGY.COM   USA

WWW.BAYDESIGNS.COM/
BAYDESIGNS | INFO@BAYDESIGNS.COM

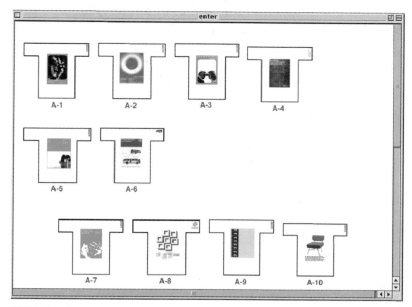

WWW.IFNET.OR.JP/~YAMAP/ENTERMAIN.HTML

JAPAN

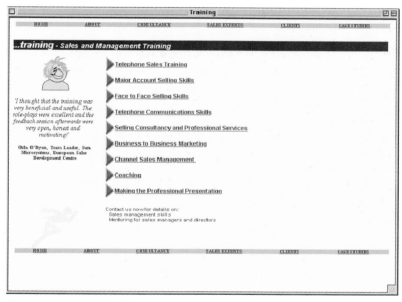

WWW.IFASSOCIATES.COM/TRAINING.HTM
PETER TURNER | TURNER & COMPANY COMMUNICATIONS | PTURNER@BTINTERNET.COM   UK

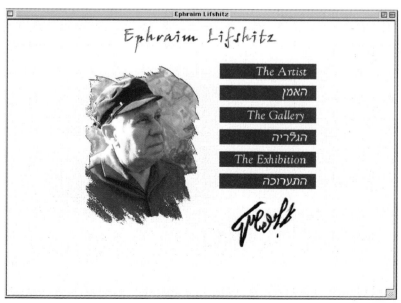

WWW.LIFSHITZ.ORG.IL/
WWW.FANTASY.CO.IL

ISRAEL

WWW.ALVR1.COM/REDFILMS
JOSEPH ALVIAR | WWW.ALVR1.COM

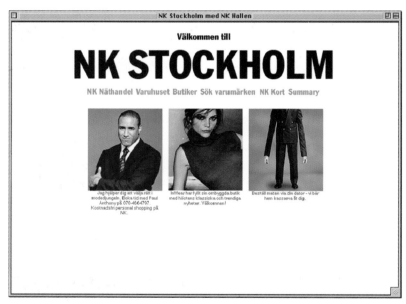

WWW.NK.SE/STOCKHOLM/INDEX.HTML   JAKOB SWEDENBORG, JOHAN EKLUND, PIJASUNDIN
SATAMA INTERACTIVE | WWW.SATAMA.COM   SWEDEN

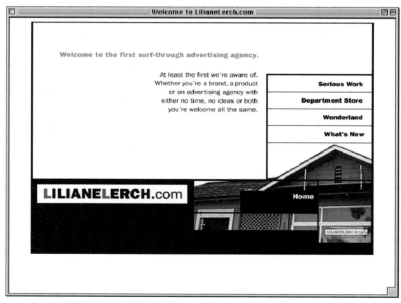

WWW.LILIANELERCH.COM/HOME.HTM
LILIANE LERCH, ALEX KOHNKE, HIPDESIGN.COM | LILIANE@LILIANELERCH.COM   USA

WWW.STREETSPACE.COM/INTRO.HTM
ANDY LIM | ANDY@ARTDIRECTORS.COM
MALAYSIA

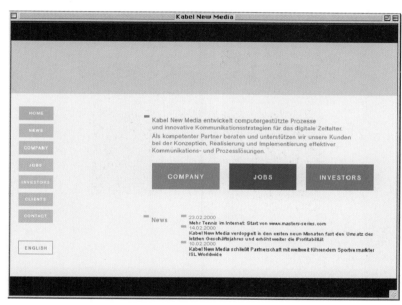

WWW.KABEL.DE/DE/HOME/TOPINHALT.HTML
MARION REICHERT | KABEL NEW MEDIA | WWW.KABEL.DE
TOM DUSCHER, ELLEN JUERGENSEN,
GERMANY

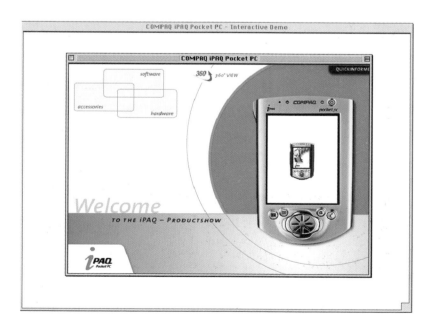

WWW.COMA2.DE/IPAQ
COLLIN CROOME | COMA2 | COLLIN@COMA2.COM
GERMANY

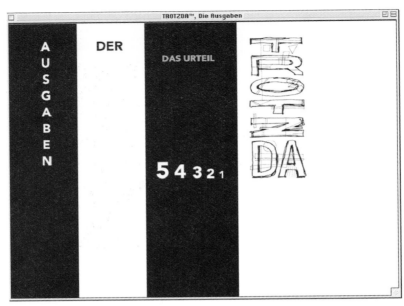

WWW.E-7.COM/~TROTZDA/MEHR
PAUL APOSTOLOU, OLIVER VIETS | ELEPHANT SEVEN GMBH | E-7.COM

GERMANY

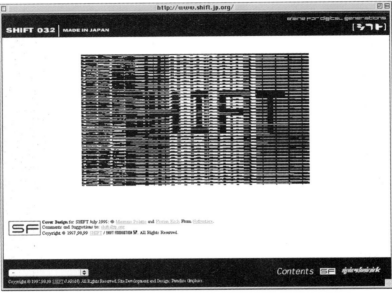

WWW.SHIFT.JP.ORG/
MAURIZIO POLETTO & FLORIAN KOCH | NOFRONTIERE | SHIFT@JP.ORG

JAPAN

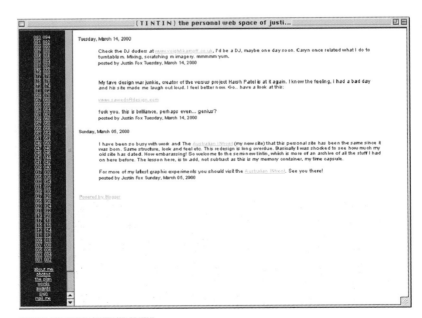

WWW.CIA.COM.AU/DFM/TINTIN/START.HTML
JUSTIN FOX | ANIMAL LOGIC PTY LTD | JUSTINF@AL.COM.AU

AUSTRALIA

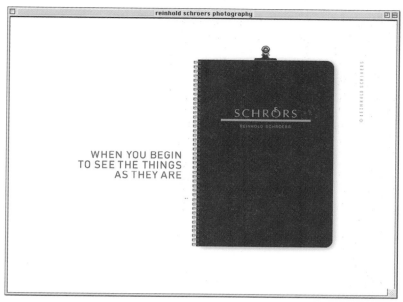

WHEN YOU BEGIN
TO SEE THE THINGS
AS THEY ARE

WWW.SCHROERS.COM/INDEX2.HTM
JOERG WASCHAT | VS.42 | WWW.VS42.COM   GERMANY

WWW.DIGITAL-EXPERIENCES.COM/
DALJIT SINGH | DIGIT | WWW.DIGIT1.COM   GERMANY

WWW.FREELENS.COM/
LUTZ FISCHMANN & GOGGI STRAUSS | FREELENS ONLINE GMBH | MAIL@FREELENS.COM   GERMANY

101

WWW.EYAD.COM/HOME.HTM
EYAD ABU TAHA | EYADEYAD.COM | EYAD@EYAD.COM

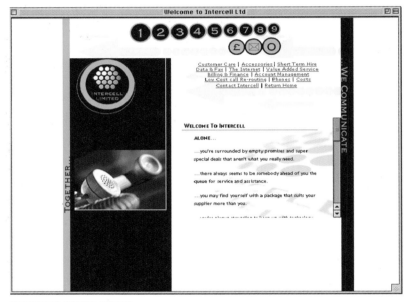

WWW.INTERCELL.CO.UK/NFL_FSET.HTML
NETWORKS | WWW.NETWORKS.CO.UK   UK

WWW.BASILISK.CH/
JOHANNES GAMPERL | INFO@JG-WEBDESIGN.DE   GERMANY

WWW.CYBERNETIC.COM.HK/CHINESE/
DOMINIC FUNG | CYBERNETIC INFORMATION TECHNOLOGY   HONG KONG

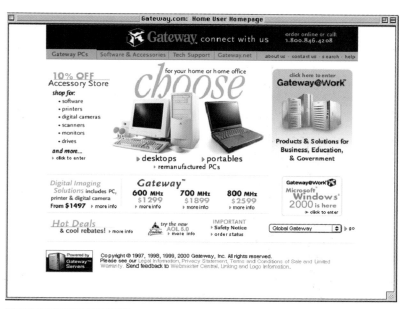

WWW.GATEWAY.COM/HOME/INDEX.SHTML

USA

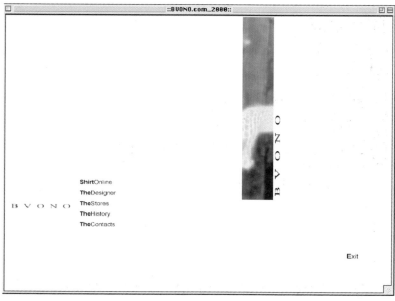

WWW.BVONO.COM/SPLASH.HTM
HYPERBROS | WWW.HYPERBROS.COM   ITALY

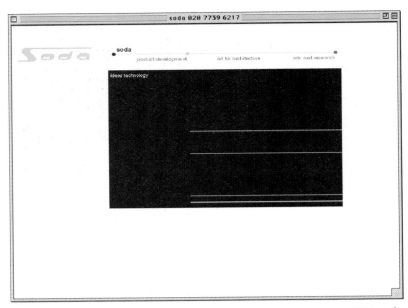

SODAPLAY.COM
SODA

UK

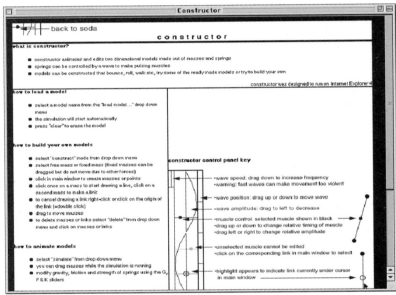

SODAPLAY.COM/CONSTRUCTOR
SODA

UK

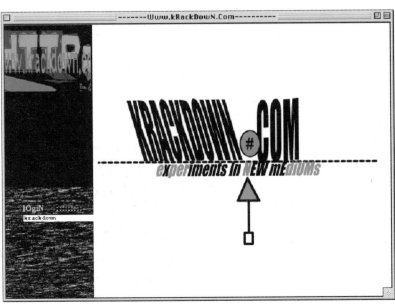

WWW.KRACKDOWN.COM/
JAMES THOMS | KRACKDOWN@KRACKDOWN.COM

USA

MEMBERS.XOOM.COM/FRIQUI/LN2/ROU
HORACIO FIEBELKORN   ARGENTINA

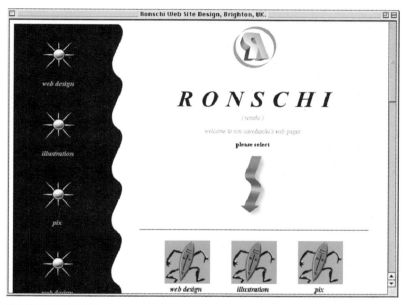

WWW.RONSCHI.DEMON.CO.UK/
RON CAVEDASCHI | RONSCHI WEB DESIGN | RON@RONSCHI.DEMON.CO.UK   UK

WWW.DJTIMES.COM/TCHOME/DJTIMES/INDEX.HTM
WWW.DJTIMES.COM | DJTIMES@TESTA.COM

WWW.ICA.ORG.UK	SIMON CRAB, DAVID JONES, SAM COLLET, SIARON HUGHES
LATERAL NET LTD. | WWW.LATERAL.NET	UK

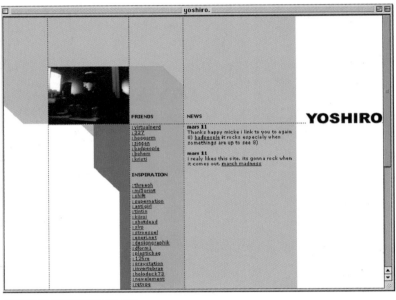

HEM.PASSAGEN.SE/POZEIDON/INDEX2.HTML
ALEXANDER PETTERSSON | ONTOYOSHIRO@RSUB.COM

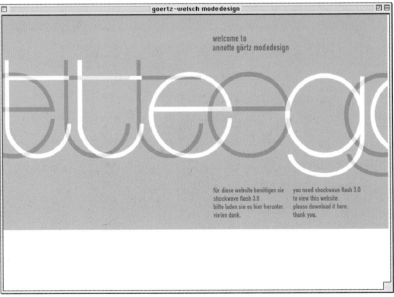

WWW.ANNETTEGOERTZ.DE/
JOERG WASCHAT |VS42 | WWW.VS42.COM	GERMANY

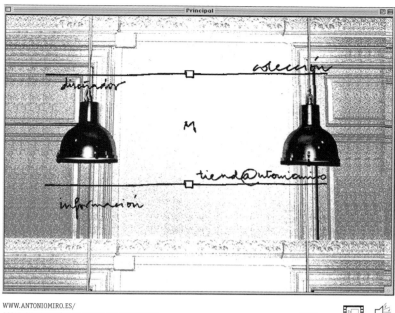

WWW.ANTONIOMIRO.ES/
OSCAR GUTIERREZ | MARKETING@ANTONIOMIRO.ES SPAIN

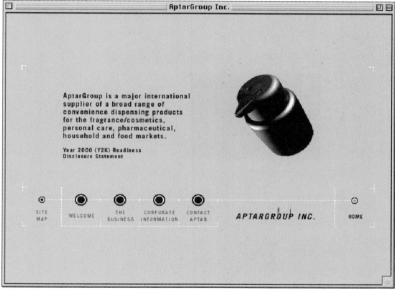

WWW.APTARGROUP.COM/HOME.HTML   RALPH POLTERMANN | APTARGROUP & PAT SAMATA,
KEVIN KRUEGER | PERFORMANCE NETWORKS | PERFORMANCENETWORKS.COM

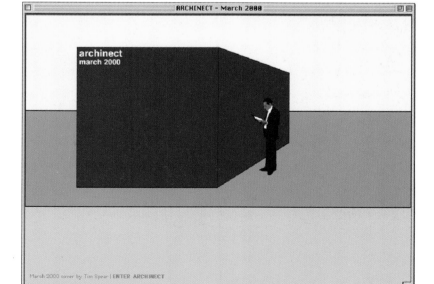

WWW.ARCHINECT.COM/INDEX_3_00.HTML
PAUL PETRUNIA, COVER BY TIM SPEAR | PAUL@ARCHINECT.COM   USA

WWW.EXPLORATORIUM.EDU
EXPLORATORIUM INTERACTIVE MEDIA TEAM | RONH@EXPLORATORIUM.EDU   USA

WWW.AUTOMATIK.DE
MARKUS HOLTHAUSEN | HOLLY@AUTOMATIK.DE   GERMANY

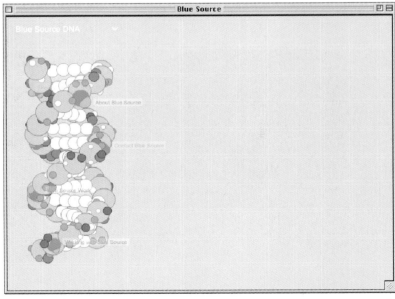

WWW.BLUESOURCE.COM/HOME_INDEX
MARK WALLIS | TONIC DESIGN LIMITED | WWW.TONICDESIGN.CO.UK   UK

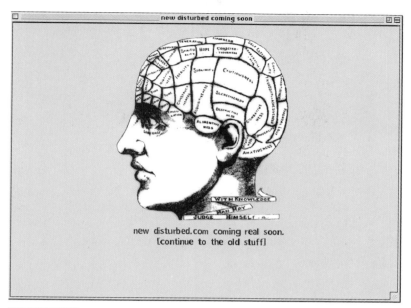

WWW.DISTURBED.COM/
MATT PETTY | MATT@DISTURBED.COM

WWW.CHIISAI.DE/
DENNIS KLEIN   GERMANY

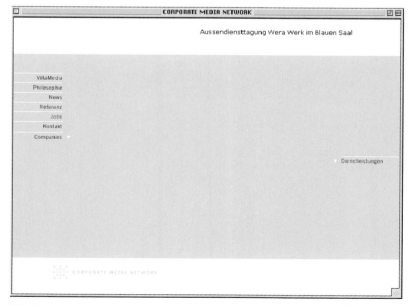

WWW.CM-NETWORK.DE/TEST/FRAME.HTML   CLEMENS LANGO, VISTAPARK DESIGNSTUDIOS &
MICHAEL RIEDEL| PUSH INTERACTIVE MEDIA GMBH | INFO@CM-NETWORK.DE   GERMANY

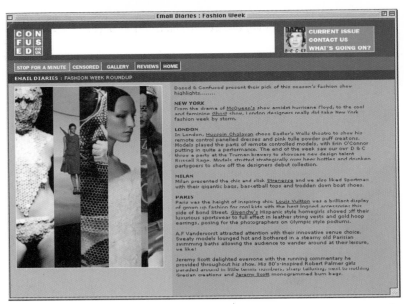

WWW.CONFUSED.CO.UK/EMAIL/INTRO.HTML
SALLY COE | FOLD7 WWW.FOLD7.COM | WWW.FOLD7.COM   UK

WWW.BURTON.COM/EXPLORE/EXPLORE.HTM
DAVE BUCKLAND, CHUCK WHITE | BURTON | INFO@BURTON.COM   USA

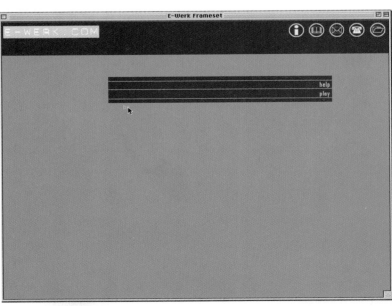

WWW.E-WERK.COM/E-WERK/FRAMESET
PAUL APOSTOLOU, OLIVER VIETS | ELEPHANT SEVEN GMBH | WWW.E-7.COM   GERMANY

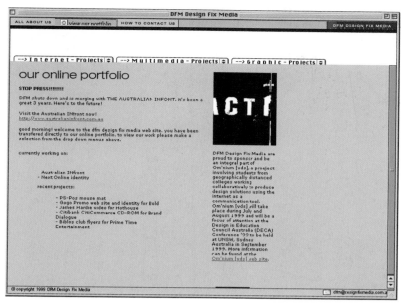

WWW.DESIGNFIXMEDIA.COM.AU/START.HTML

JUSTIN FOX | ANIMAL LOGIC PTY LTD | JUSTINF@AL.COM.AU   AUSTRALIA

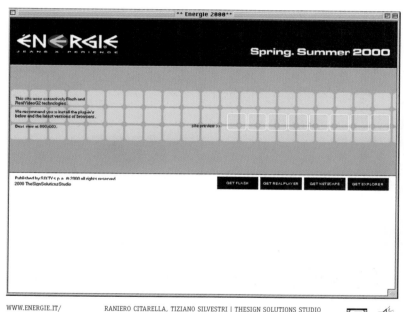

WWW.ENERGIE.IT/   RANIERO CITARELLA, TIZIANO SILVESTRI | THESIGN SOLUTIONS STUDIO
WWW.THESIGNSOLUTIONS.COM   ITALY

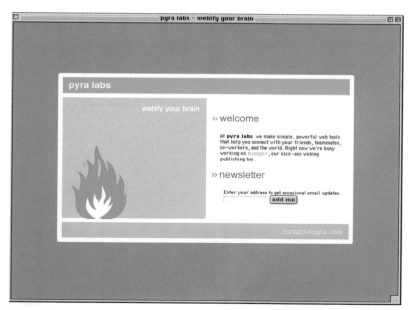

WWW.PYRA.COM
PYRA LABS

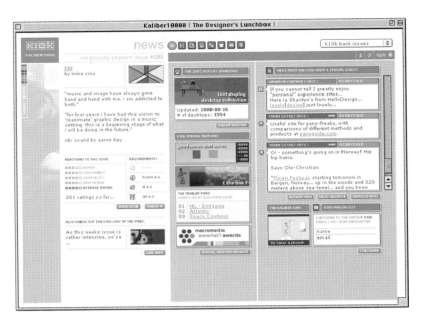

WWW.K10K.NET/
MICHAEL SCHMIDT, TOKE NYGAARD| KALIBER10000 | SPEAK@K10K.NET   DENMARK

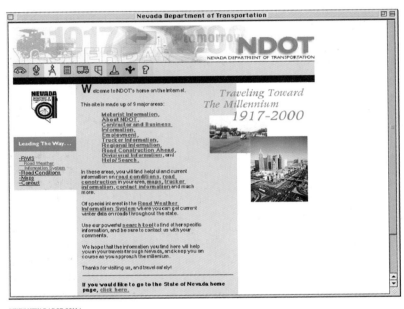

WWW.NEVADADOT.COM/
TECHINFO@NEVADADOT.COM   USA

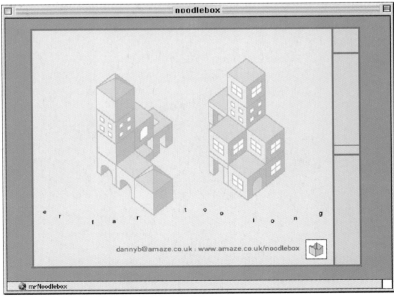

WWW.NOODLEBOX.COM/CLASSIC/INDEX.HTML
DANIEL BROWN / AMAZE LIMITED | DANNYB@AMAZE.COM   UK

WWW.RECOM.DE
THORSTEN "JASPER" WEESE

GERMANY

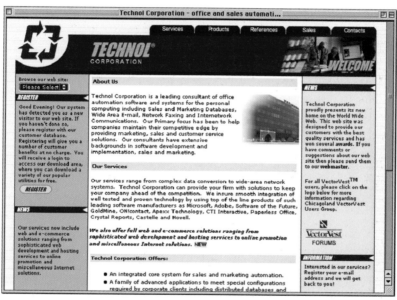

WWW.TECHNOLCORP.COM
ANDREW A. KUCHERIAVY | INTECHNIC CORPORATION | ANDREW@INTECHNIC.COM

USA

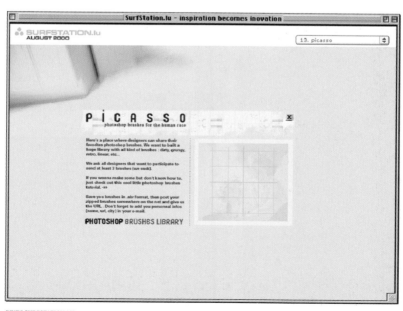

WWW.SURFSTATION.LU
GERMÁN OLAYA

COLOMBIA

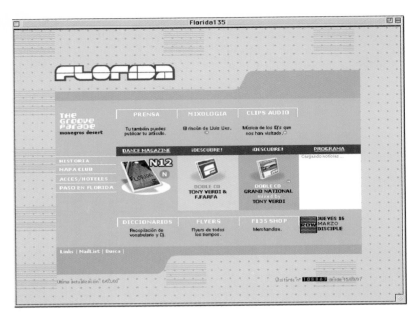

WWW.FLORIDA135.COM/

SPAIN

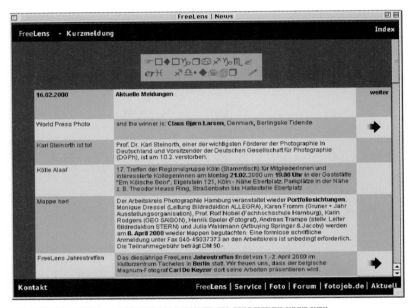

WWW.FREELENS.COM/NEWS/   LUTZ FISCHMANN & GOGGI STRAUSS; BEIDE FREELENS ONLINE GMBH
MAIL@FREELENS.COM   GERMANY

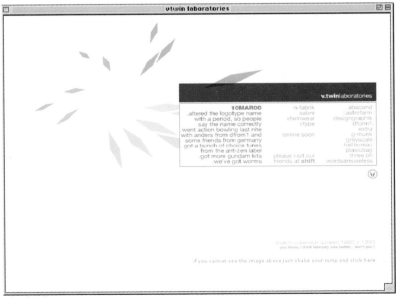

WWW.VTWINLABS.COM/
JASON RUDDY | V.TWIN LABORATORIES | VTWINALPHA@VTWINLABS.COM

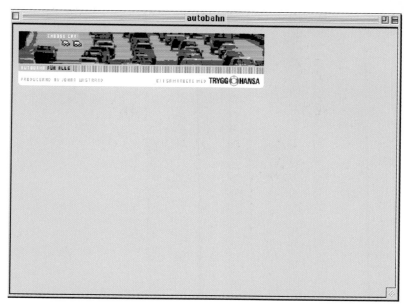

WWW.HONUNG.SE/AUTOBAHN/
JOHAN WISTRAND | JOHAN.WISTRAND@HONUNG.SE   SWEDEN

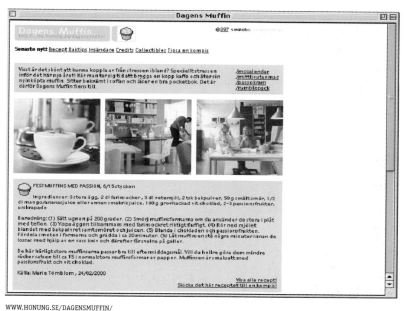

WWW.HONUNG.SE/DAGENSMUFFIN/
JOHAN WISTRAND | JOHAN.WISTRAND@HONUNG.SE   SWEDEN

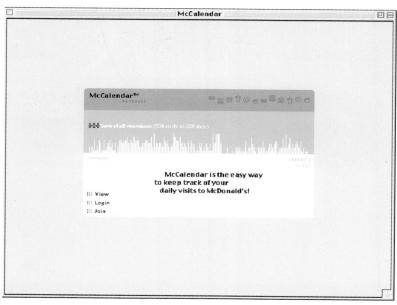

WWW.HONUNG.SE/MCCALENDAR/
JOHAN WISTRAND | JOHAN.WISTRAND@HONUNG.SE   SWEDEN

117

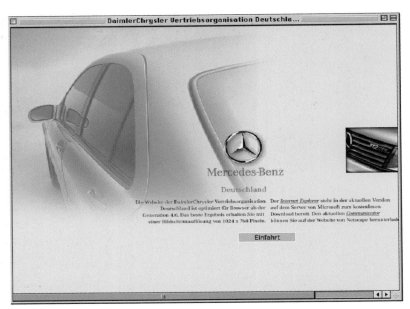

WWW.MERCEDES-BENZ.DE/

GERMANY

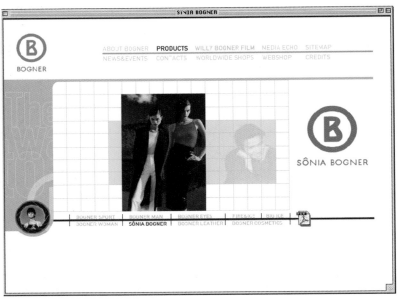

WWW.BOGNER.COM/ENGLISH/PRODUCTS/KSONIA.HTML
PERPLEX | INFO@PERPLEX.DE

GERMANY

WWW.SMART.COM

WWW.ONYRO.COM/MARIANTHI
ANTHONY KYRIAZIS | KIOKEN UK | WWW.ONYRO.COM/
UK

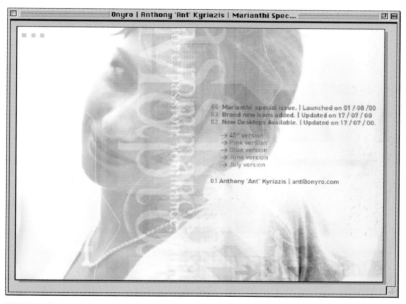

WWW.ONYRO.COM/MARIANTHI
ANTHONY KYRIAZIS | KIOKEN UK | WWW.ONYRO.COM/
UK

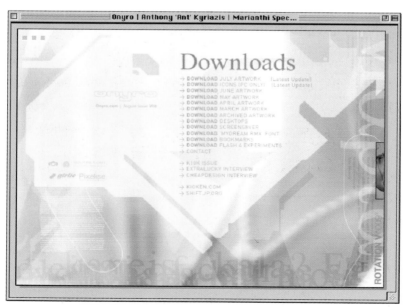

WWW.ONYRO.COM/MARIANTHI/3
ANTHONY KYRIAZIS | KIOKEN UK | WWW.ONYRO.COM/
UK

SPACEFLIGHT.NASA.GOV
KIM DISMUKES, KELLY HUMPHRIES | NASA HUMAN SPACE FLIGHT WEB USA

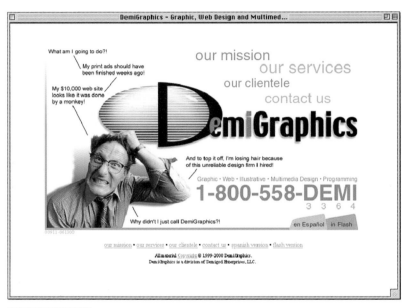

WWW.DEMIGRAPHICS.COM/
BRIAN SANCHEZ | DEMIGRAPHICS.COM | NFO@DEMIGRAPHICS.COM USA

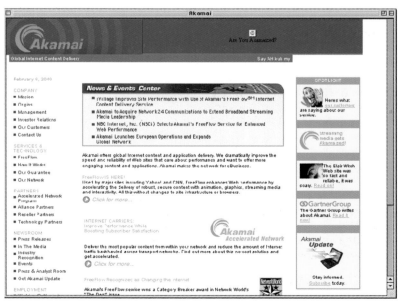

WWW.AKAMAI.COM/HOME.SHTML

WWW.AIWA.COM/COMPANY.ASP

USA

WWW.AIR-EUROPA.COM/AEA/
MIGUEL RIVAVELARDE | ICON MEDIALAB MADRID | MIGUEL@ICONMEDIALAB.ES

SPAIN

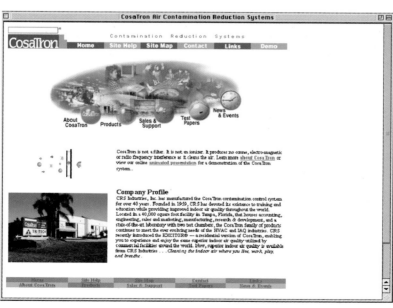

WWW.COSATRON.COM/
LINDA PEDERSEN | CYBERELF, INC. | WWW.CYBERELF.COM

USA

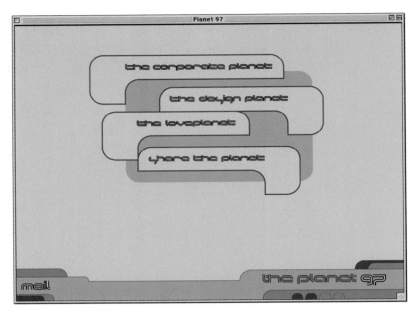

WWW.PLANET.DK/97_INDEX.HTML

THE PLANET MULTIMEDIA DESIGN STUDIO | BEAM@PLANET.DK   DENMARK

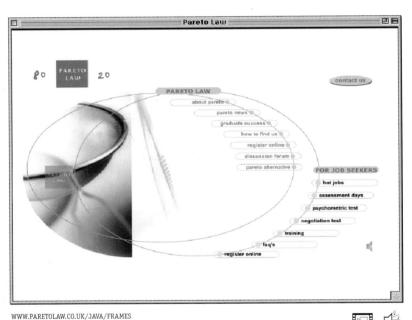

WWW.PARETOLAW.CO.UK/JAVA/FRAMES

INFO@PARETOLAW.CO.UK   UK

WWW.EZHE.RU/PRAVDA/INDEX.HTML

RUSSIA

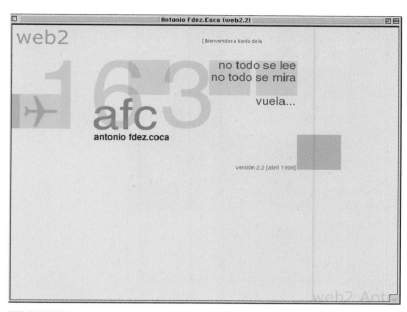

MCCD.UDC.ES/COCA/
ANTONIO FERNÁNDEZ COCA | WWW.FERNANDEZCOCA.COM   SPAIN

WWW.ALKARMEL.ORG/
EYAD ABU TAHA | INTERTECH PALESTINE

WWW.SIERRAPACIFIC.COM/
DONNA R. SMIT & AZTECH CYBERSPACE | DAVEL@AZTECH-CS.COM   USA

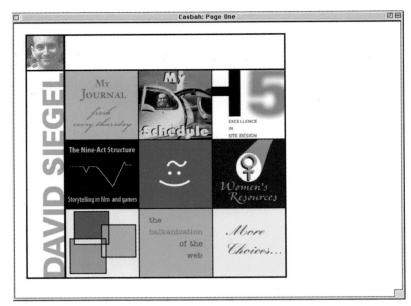

WWW.DSIEGEL.COM/CASBAH/OPTION3/QUILT3.1.HTML
DAVID SIEGEL | LIST@DSIEGEL.COM   USA

WWW.BSTATTOO.COM.AU/

AUSTRALIA

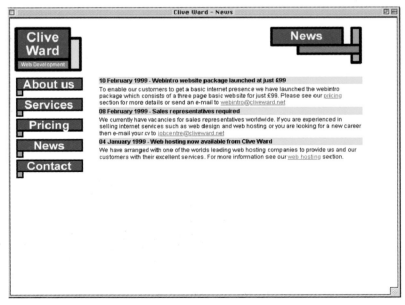

WWW.CLIVEWARD.NET/NEWS.HTM
CLIVE@CLIVEWARD.NET

WWW.CHINAPRO.COM/

USA

WWW.BCN.ES/CASTELLA/EHOME.HTM
BARCELONA CITY COUNCIL | BI@MAIL.BCN.ES

SPAIN

WWW.ENRON.COM/

WWW.KALLKWIK.CO.UK/
DOMINO SYSTEMS | WWW.DOMINO.COM   UK

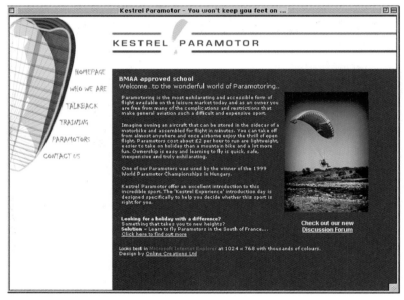

WWW.KESTRELPARAMOTOR.CO.UK/
ANDREW BAILEY | OCULA LTD   UK

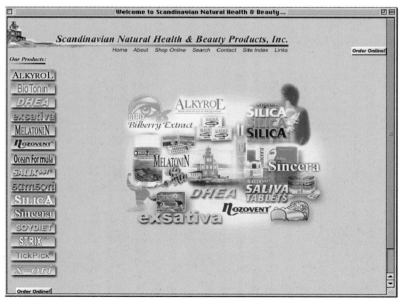

SCANDINAVIANNATURALS.COM
JEFF HOBRATH ART STUDIO | HEALTH@SCANDINAVIANNATURALS.COM   USA

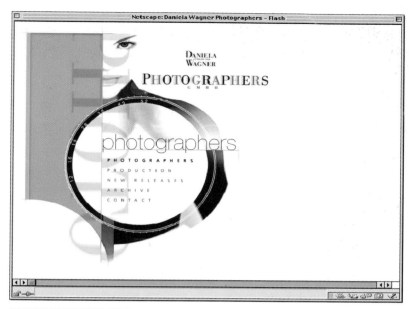

WWW.PHOTOGRAPHERS.DE/FRAME.HTML
COLLIN CROOME | COMA2 | COLLIN@COMA2.COM   GABON

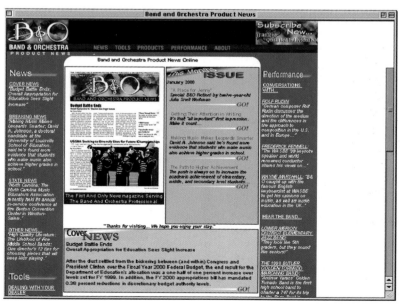

WWW.LUKAS-KRANKENHAUS.DE/
RULLKOETTER AGD | WWW.RULLKOETTER.DE   GERMANY

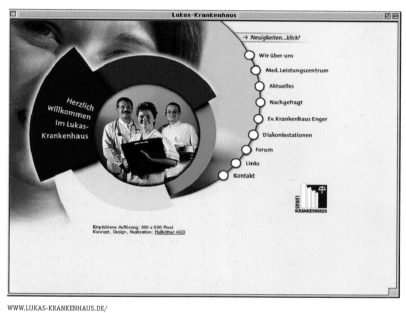

WWW.BANDANDORCHESTRA.COM/TCHOME/BO/INDEX.HTM
CHRISTIAN UGOLINI |TESTA PUBLICATIONS | CUGOLINI@TESTA.COM

WWW.INTERNET-PROMOTIONS.CO.UK/

UK

WWW.BATES.DE/SMALL/INDEX.HTM
IVAR LEON MENGER, ANDREAS HEINZEL | KEIMKRAFT DESIGN | BATES@BATES.DE

GERMANY

WWW.DESIGNGRAPHIK.COM/DE/INDEX2.HTML
MIKE YOUNG | EPYT | MIKE@DESIGNGRAPHIK.COM

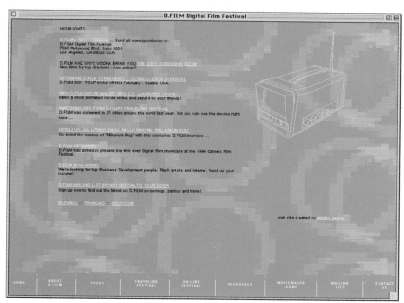

HIGHLIGHTS:

D.FILM NEWSLETTER ... Send all correspondence to:
D.FILM Digital Film Festival
7095 Hollywood Blvd. Suite 1001
Los Angeles, CA 90028 USA

D.FILM AND SKYY VODKA BRING YOU THE SKYY SCREENING ROOM
New films by top directors - now online!

UPCOMING D.FILM SCREENINGS - GLOBALLY-LOCK >> DIGITAL
D.FILM 2000° TOUR kicks off this February - Seattle USA

NEW D.FILM MOVIE MAKER VERSION 2.0 - LAUNCHES SOON!
Make a short animated movie online and send it to your friends!

WATCH MOVIES FROM D.FILM'S TRAVELING FESTIVAL
D.FILM was screened in 21 cities around the world last year. But you can see the movies right here ...

BINGE-LINK D.FILMS TALKS SHOW MOVING THE D.FILM BUG
Go behind the scenes of "Millenium Bug" with this exclusive D.FILM interview ...

D.FILM AT CANNES
D.FILM was asked to present the first ever Digital Film showcase at the 1999 Cannes Film Festival.

D.FILM NOW HIRING
We're looking for top Business Development people, Flash artists and interns. Send us your resume!

D.FILM MAILING LIST BRINGS DIGITAL TO YOUR DOOR
Sign up now to find out the latest on D.FILM screenings, parties and more!

ESPAÑOL :: FRANÇAIS :: DEUTSCHE

web site created by shinko design

| HOME | ABOUT D.FILM | PRESS | TRAVELING FESTIVAL | ON-LINE FESTIVAL | RESOURCES | MOVIEMAKER GAME | MAILING LIST | CONTACT US |

WWW.DFILM.COM/HOME.HTML
BEN RIGBY, ARDITH IBANEZ RIGBY, BART CHEEVER | INFO@DFILM.COM

USA

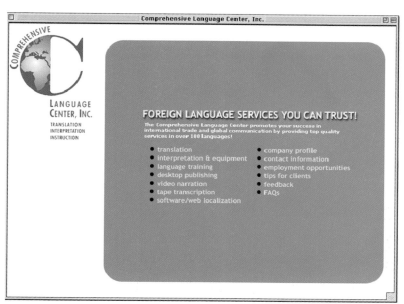

WWW.COMLANG.COM/

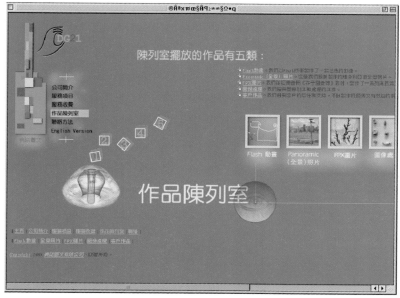

WWW.DG21.COM/SHOWCASE-C.HTM
DIGITALONE LTD. | WWW.DG21.COM

HONG KONG

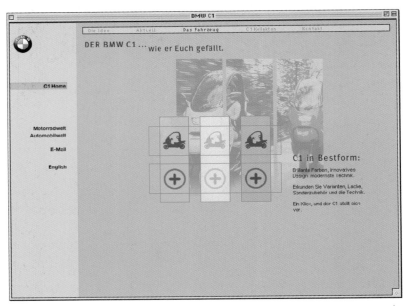

WWW.BIKE.BMW.COM/C1
A.F.I.M. | DORIT.RUPE@BMW.DE
GERMANY

NEW-YEARS-EVE.CO.UK/
YVONNE FAGE, NETHEADER
UK

WWW.BLUEFLY.COM/

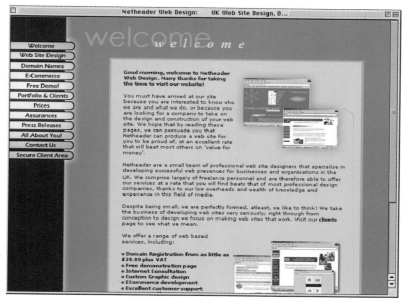

WWW.NETHEADER.NET/
NETHEADER WEB DESIGN | INFO@NETHEADER.NET   UK

WWW.DAYSTREAM.COM/
BENJI ADAMS | DAYSTREAM WEB DEVELOPERS, LLC.

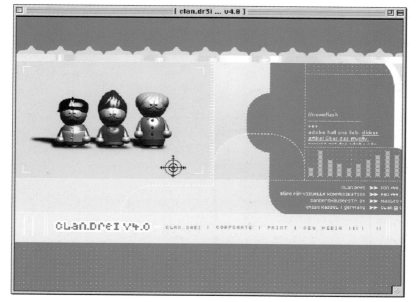

WWW.CLANDREI.DE/
KAI BRUNNING, LARS RÜCKERT | CLAN.DREI | CLAN@CLANDREI.DE   GERMANY

WWW.BENETTON.COM/COLORS/ISSUES/MONOCULTURE36/INDEX.HTML

ITALY

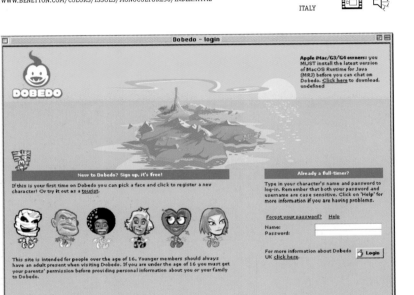

WWW.DOBEDO.CO.UK/
INFO@DOBEDO-IN.COM

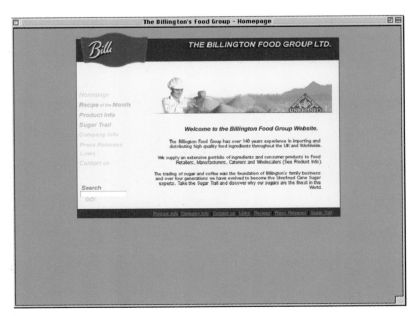

WWW.BILLINGTONS.CO.UK/
AMAZE | WWW.AMAZE.COM

UK

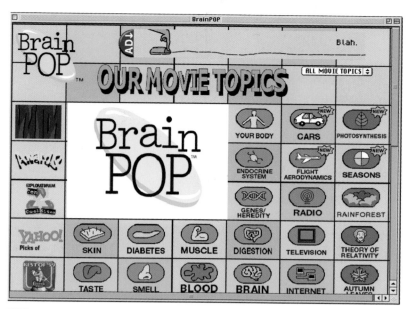

WWW.BRAINPOP.COM/INDEXGEN.ASP
BRAINPOP.COM

USA

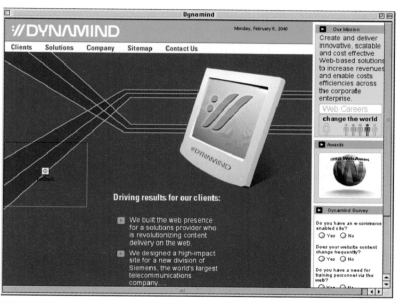

WWW.DMIND.COM
CHAD GURLEY | DMIND CORPORATION | INFO@DMIND.COM

USA

WWW.DPHK.ORG/

HONG KONG

WWW.COLUMBIA.EDU/~ALS3/SPLINTER.HTML

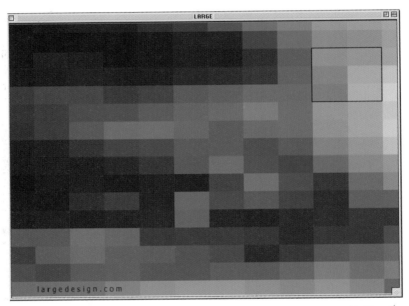

WWW.LARGEDESIGN.COM/
LARS HEMMING JORGENSEN | LARGE DESIGN LIMITED

UK

WWW.MALAYSIA-WEB.COM/CSN/

MALAYSIA

WWW.DEUTSCHE-BANK-24.DE   DIE ARGONAUTEN | W WW.ARGONAUTEN.DE & SINNERSCHRADER
WWW.SINNERSCHRADER.DE | INFO@DB24.DE   GERMANY

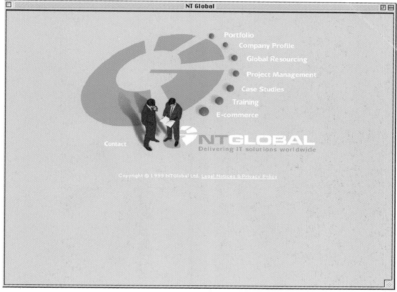

WWW.NTGLOBAL.NET/

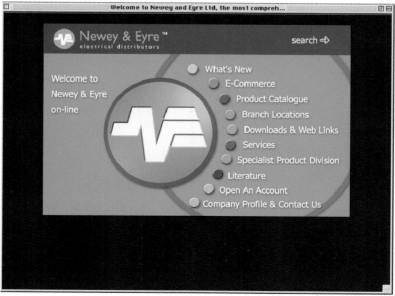

WWW.NEWEYANDEYRE.CO.UK/
NEWEY & EYRE | WAX DIGITAL | WWW.WAX-DIGITAL.COM   UK

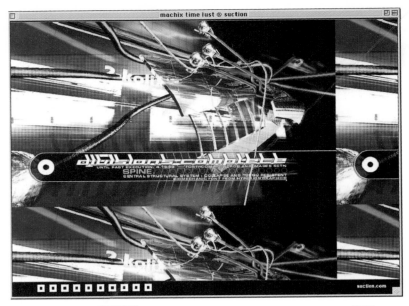

WWW.SUCTION.COM/MACHIX/INDEX.HTML
EDDIE PAK | SUCTION | EPAK@SUCTION.COM   USA

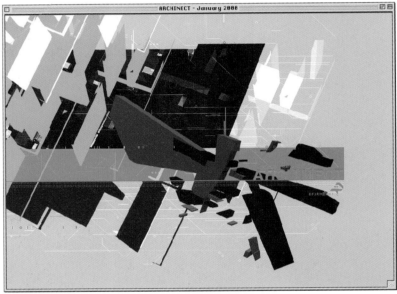

WWW.ARCHINECT.COM/INDEX_1_00.HTML
PAUL PETRUNIA, COVER BY WWW.DFORM1.NET | PAUL@ARCHINECT.COM   USA

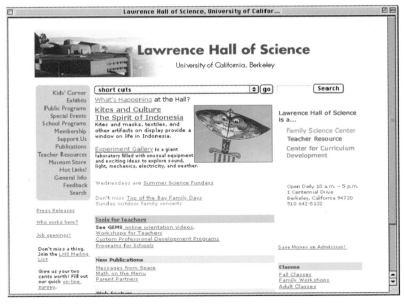

WWW.LHS.BERKELEY.EDU
SARA LEAVITT | LAWRENCE HALL OF SCIENCE | NEWSCENTER@PA.UREL.BERKELEY.EDU   USA

WWW.VPRO.NL/FRONTEND/INDEX.SHTML

NETHERLANDS

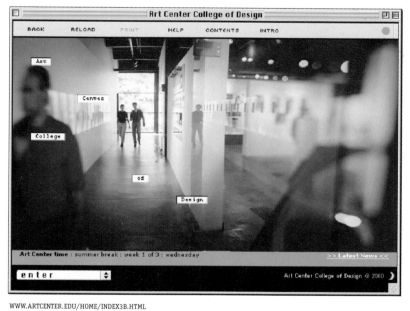

WWW.ARTCENTER.EDU/HOME/INDEX3B.HTML
STEPHEN NOWLIN | ART CENTER COLLEGE OF DESIGN

USA

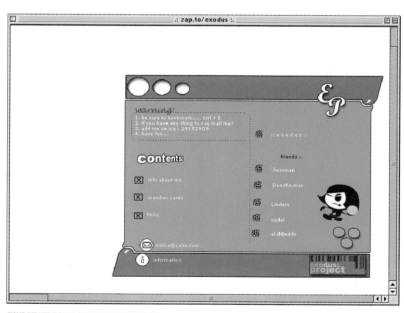

HOME.BIP.NET/BRITTA.SELIN/EXODUS/MAIN.HTM
MIKAEL SELIN | MIKKE@SELIN.COM

SWEDEN

WWW.NETBABYWORLD.COM/

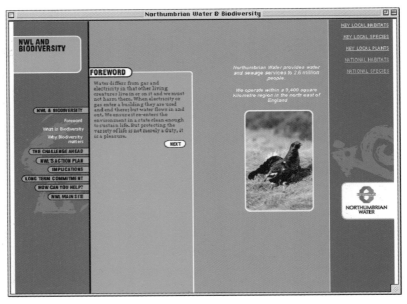

WWW.NWL.CO.UK/BIODIVERSITY/

UK

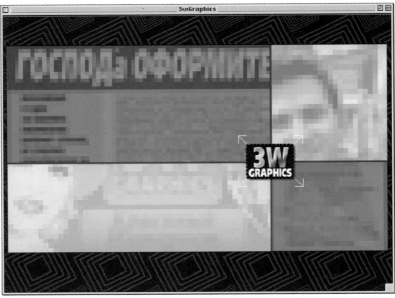

WWW.3WGRAPHICS.COM/START2.HTML

RUSSIA

WWW.PADDINGTONBEAR.CO.UK/
PADDINGTON AND CO. LTD. 2000 | KABEL NEW MEDIA BRIGHTON   UK

WWW.PETER-HOPPE.COM/HTML/SPLASH.HTML
RULLKOETTER AGD | WWW.RULLKOETTER.DE   GERMANY

WWW.LOUVRE.FR/

FRANCE

WWW.KOBRA.NET/WAITING/
MAGNUS HÖGGREN | MAGNUS@KOBRA.NET

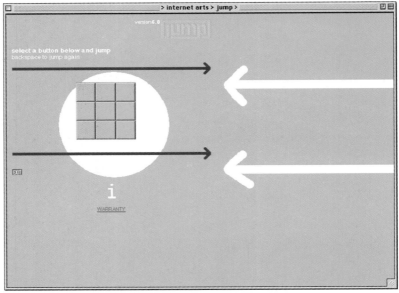

WWW.THECOOKER.COM/HERE/JUMP.HTML
JAKE TILSON | ©ATLAS 1994-2000 | JAKE@THECOOKER.COM   USA

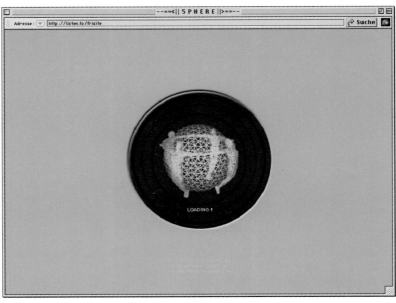

LISTEN.TO/FRISITE
CALLE GRÖNLUND | FRISITE@KASTEMA.TO

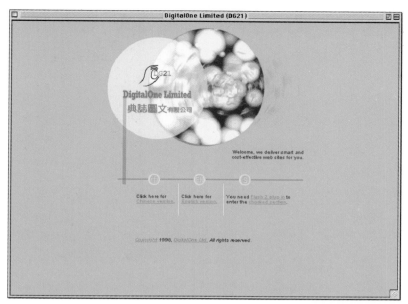

WWW.DG21.COM/
DIGITALONE LTD. | WWW.DG21.COM

HONG KONG

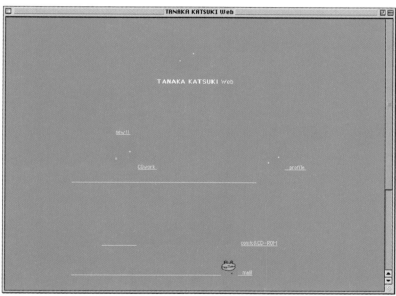

WWW.MULTIES.CO.JP/~KA2KI/KWEB/KWEB_INDEX.HTML

JAPAN

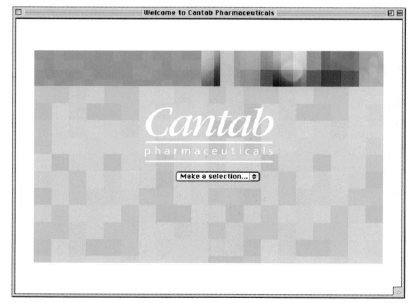

WWW.CANTAB.CO.UK/
DEEP CREATIVE LIMITED | WWW.DEEP.CO.UK

UK

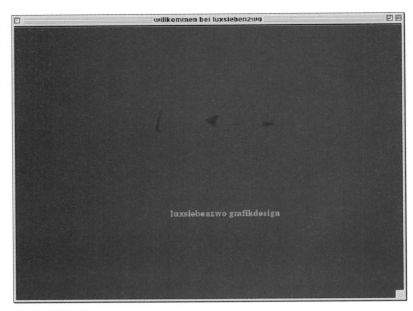

WWW.LUXSIEBENZWO.DE/
WILLI HÖLZEL   GERMANY

WWW.BABYLONZOO.CO.UK/
GRAHAM KNIGHT | INFO@BROADBAND.CO.UK   UK

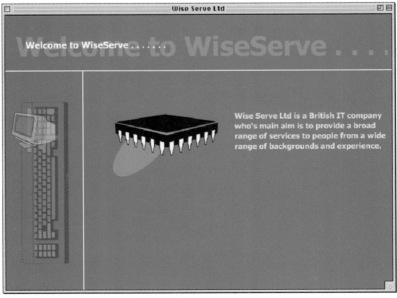

WWW.BABYLONZOO.CO.UK/
GRAHAM KNIGHT | BROADBAND | INFO@BROADBAND.CO.UK   UK

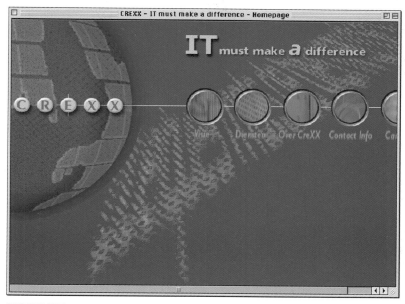

WWW.CREXX.COM/
RUUD VENDELOO | CREXX GREEN B.V. | WWW.VISIONWEB.COM   NETHERLANDS

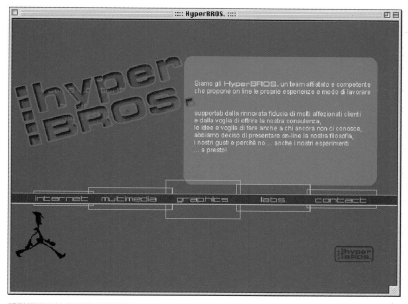

WWW.HYPERBROS.COM/HYPERMAIN.HTM
HYPERBROS   ITALY

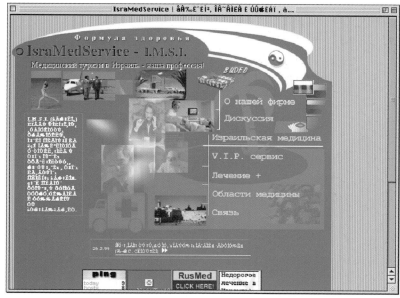

WWW.ISRAMEDSERVICE.COM/
WEBPROM DESIGN | WWW.WEB-DESIGN.CO.IL   ISRAEL

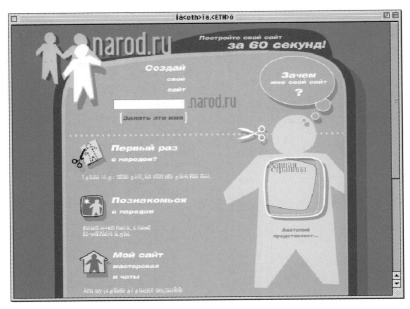

WWW.NAROD.RU/

WWW.MERSEYSIDE.ORG.UK/LO_START.
AMAZE | HELEN.HODGES@MERSEYSIDE.ORG.U

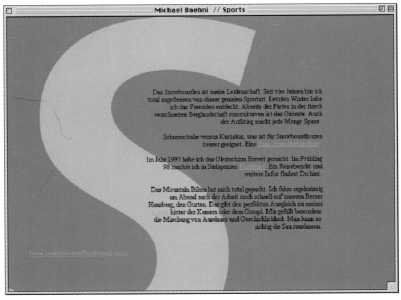

WWW.APPROX.CH/PRIVAT/SPORTS.HTML
MICHAEL BÄHNI | INFO@APPROX.CH

WWW.RAILION.NL/
BRADLEY DUNN KLERKS |INTEREDGE BV NETHERLANDS

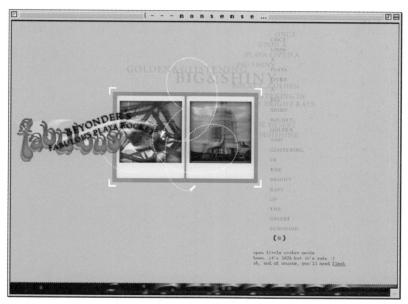

WWW.REDBEAN.COM/NONSENSE/ROCKET/ROCKET_F.HTM

WWW.SCHIESSER.DE/HOME.HTM
COLLIN CROOME | COMA2 | | COLLIN@COMA2.COM GERMANY

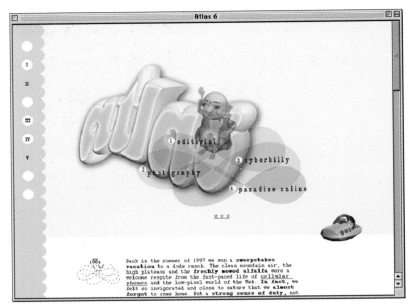

WWW.ATLASMAGAZINE.COM/   AMY FRANCESCHINI, OLIVIER LAUDE, MICHAEL MACRONE
FUTUREFARMERS | WWW.FUTUREFARMERS.COM   USA

WWW.NOODLEBOX.COM/
DANIEL BROWN / AMAZE LIMITED | DANNYB@AMAZE.COM   UK

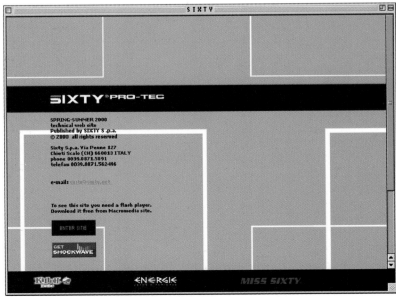

WWW.SIXTY.NET/   RANIERO CITARELLA, TIZIANO SILVESTRI | THESIGN SOLUTIONS STUDIO
WWW.THESIGNSOLUTIONS.COM | WWW.THESIGNSOLUTIONS.COM   ITALY

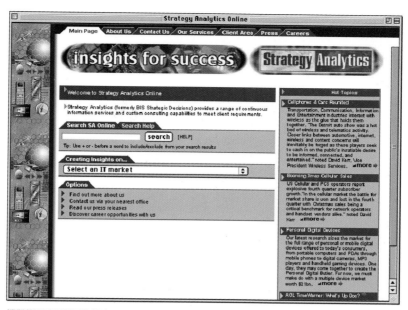

WWW.STRATEGYANALYTICS.COM/
HEXAGON MARKETING LTD | WWW.HEXNET.CO.UK   UK

WWW.MOREMILES.COM/LHCARD/INDEX.HTML
                                                            GERMANY

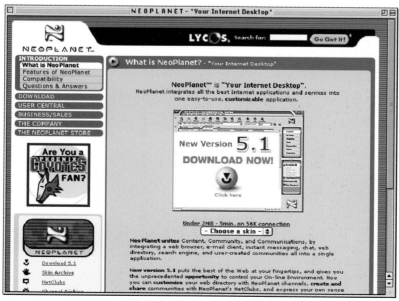

WWW.NEOPLANET.COM/
HELP@NEOPLANET.COM

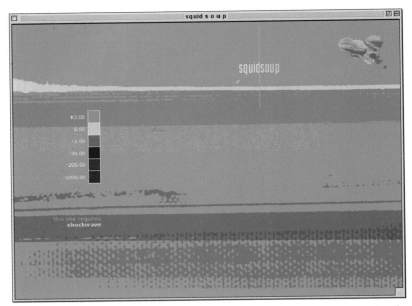

WWW.SQUIDSOUP.COM/
SQUID S O U P | MAIL@SQUIDSOUP.COM   UK

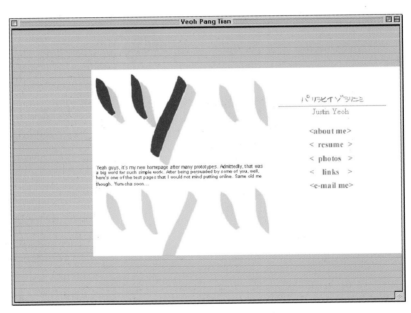

PWP.MAXIS.NET.MY/JUSTIN
YEOH PANG TIAN AKA JUSTIN | JUSTIN@MAXIS.NET.MY   MALAYSIA

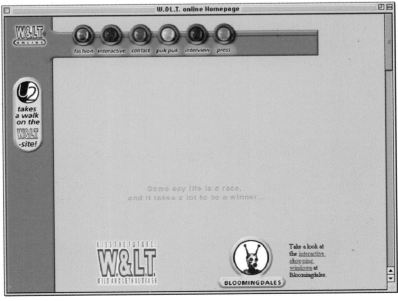

WWW.WALT.DE/

GERMANY

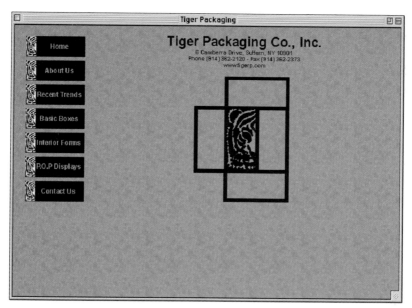

WWW.TIGERP.COM/
DUGAN CONCEPTS LLC | WWW.DUGANCONCEPTS.COM   USA

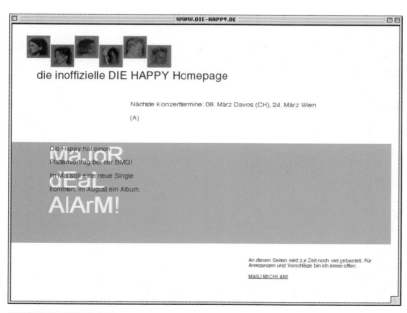

WWW.TOASTMAG.COM/
RHEN@ROADKILL.DE   USA

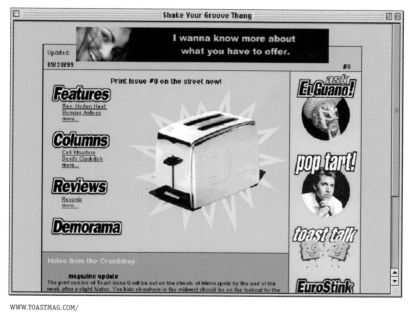

WWW.DIE-HAPPY.DE/INDEX2.HTM
RALPH RIEKER, THORSTEN MEWES | HAPPY ADVERTISING | WWW.DIEHAPPY.DE   GERMANY

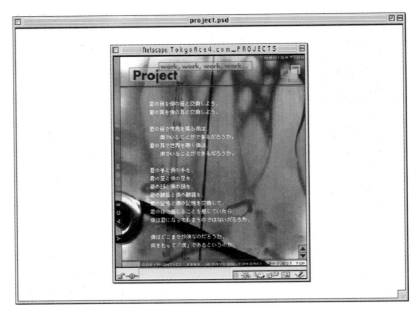

WWW.TOKYOACE4.COM/MAINMENU.CGI
TOHSAKI HISAYOSHI | Y-SAKAI@J-PAL.NE.JP   JAPAN

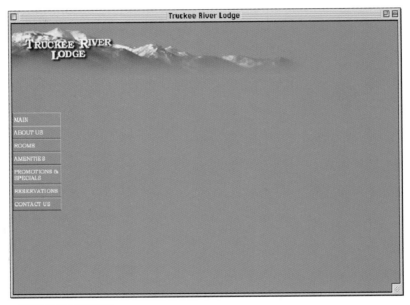

WWW.TRUCKEERIVERLODGE.COM/
MARTIN GASTANAGA PHYSICAL | AZTECH CYBERSPACE INC. | WWW.AZTECH-CS.COM   USA

WWW.ULENDORF.DK/
ULENDORF'S M&M APS | INFO@ULENDORF.DK   DENMARK

WWW.VIRUS1.NET/INDEX.HTM
MICHAEL SCHMIDT | VIRUS.ONE | INFO@VIRUS1.DK   DENMARK

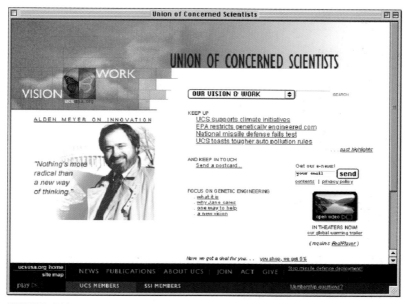

WWW.UCSUSA.ORG/
MIXIT PRODUCTIONS | WWW.MIXITPRODUCTIONS.COM   USA

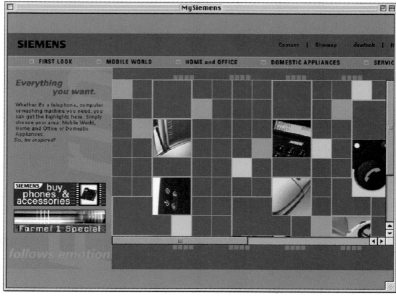

WWW.SIEMENS.COM/MYSIEMENS/ENGLISH/INDEX.HTML

                                                    GERMANY

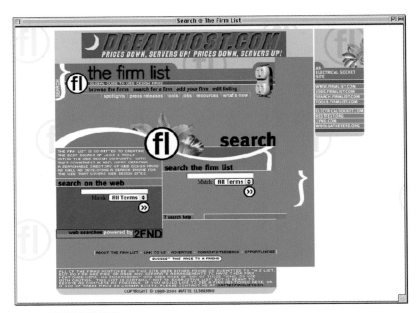

WWW.FIRMLIST.COM/MAIN.SHTML
MATTE ELSBERND | ELECTRICALSOCKET.COM   SWEDEN

SEARCH.FIRMLIST.COM
MATTE ELSBERND | ELECTRICALSOCKET.COM   SWEDEN

WWW.SIGSUG.CO.IL/
VIVID MANAGEMENT SYSTEMS | WWW.VIVID.CO.IL   ISRAEL

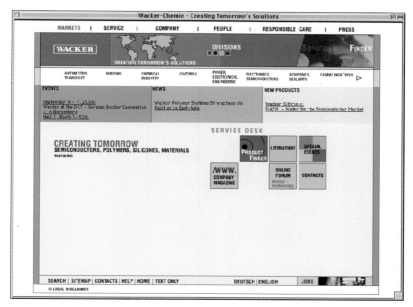

WWW.WACKER.COM
ANDREAS POULAKIDAS | WWW.PIXELPARK.COM

JENS FISCHER, CARSTEN LILGE, JULIANE JACOBI,
GERMANY

WWW.WINONA-DOT.COM/VDC
JOE NAVIN | WINONA-DOT.COM

UK

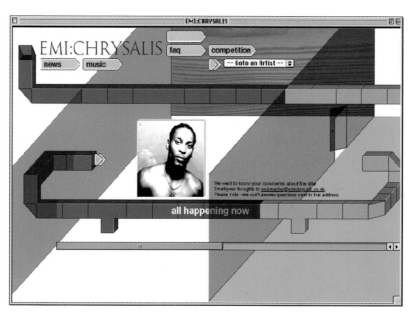

WWW.EMINATION.CO.UK/HOLDER.HTML
SIARON HUGHES | LATERAL NET LTD. | WWW.LATERAL.NET

SIMON CRAB, DAVID JONES, SAM COLLET,
UK

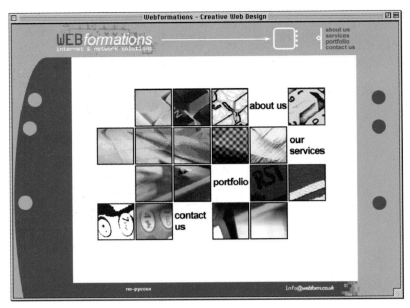

WWW.WEBFORM.CO.UK/INTRO.HTM

UK

WWW.WEBINSURANCE.ES
DISCOVERYNET | RC@DISCOVERYNET.ES

SPAIN

WWW.WIDEMEDIA.COM/FASHIONUK/
CONTACT@WIDEMEDIA.CO

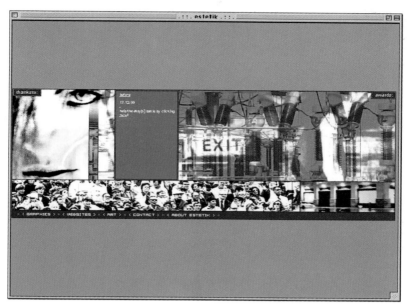

WWW.XS4ALL.NL/~ALLERT/MAIN.HTML
PETER VAN ALLER | ESTETIK@XS4ALL.NL   NETHERLANDS

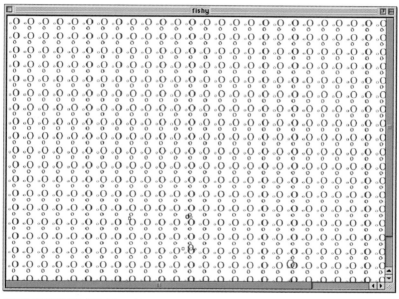

WWW.XS4ALL.NL/~LEEGTE/FISHY/FISHY.HTML
JAN ROBERT LEEGTE   NETHERLANDS

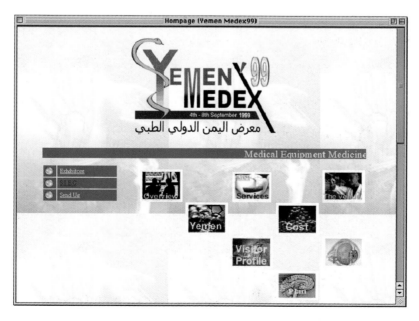

YEMEN

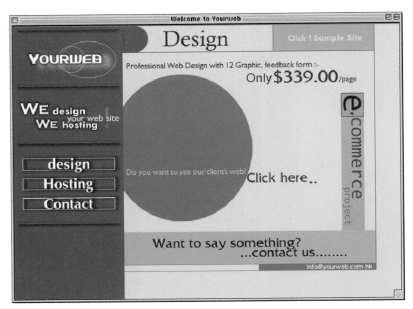

WWW.YOURWEB.COM.HK/DESIGN.HTML

HONG KONG

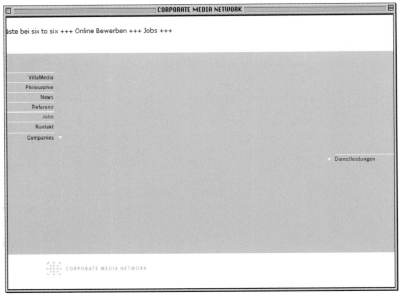

WWW.CM-NETWORK.DE/TEST/PUSH/   CHRISTOPH HONISCH, MICHAEL RIEDEL
            PUSH INTERACTIVE MEDIA GMBH & CLEMENS LANGO | VISTAPARK DESIGNSTUDIOS

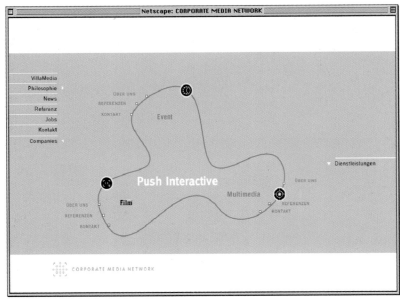

WWW.PUSH-INTERACTIVE.DE   CHRISTOPH HONISCH, MICHAEL RIEDEL
PUSH INTERACTIVE MEDIA GMBH & CLEMENS LANGO | VISTAPARK DESIGNSTUDIOS   GERMANY

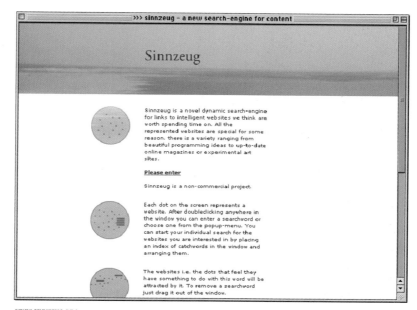

WWW.SINNZEUG.DE/
SINNZEUG@SINNZEUG.DE

GERMANY

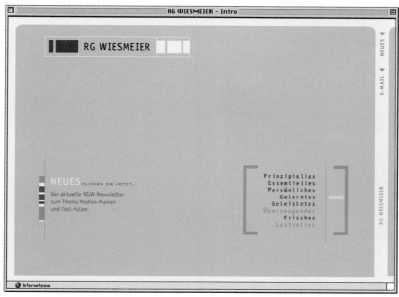

WWW.WIESMEIER.DE/
COLLIN CROOME | COMA2 | COLLIN@COMA2.COM

GERMANY

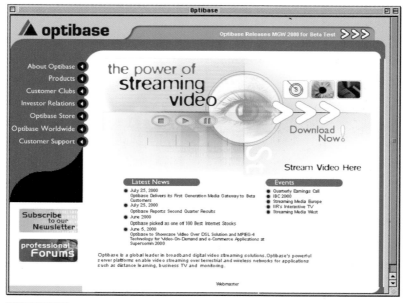

WWW.OPTIBASE.COM
SCEPIA STUDIO | WWW.SCEPIA.COM

ISRAEL

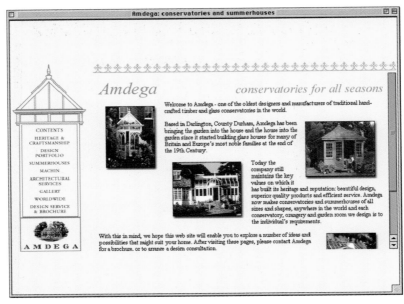

WWW.AMDEGA.COM/F-SITE.HTM
ZEBRA COMMUNICATIONS | WWW.ZEBRA.CO.UK   UK

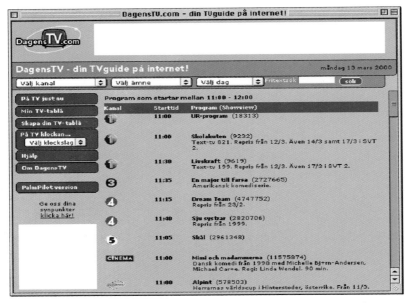

WWW.BETTERCOMM.COM/
PYI@BETTERCOMM.COM

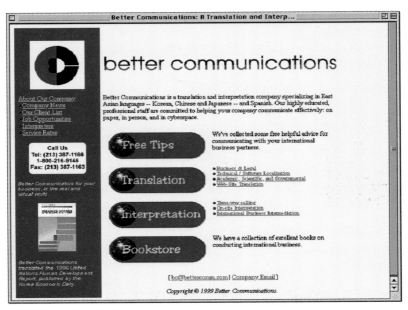

WWW.BETTERCOMM.COM/
PYI@BETTERCOMM.COM   UK

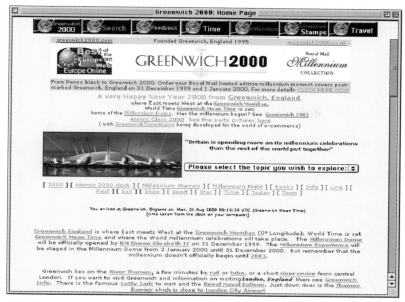

GREENWICH2000.COM/
GREENWICH 2000 LIMITED | SALES@GREENWICH2000.COM   UK

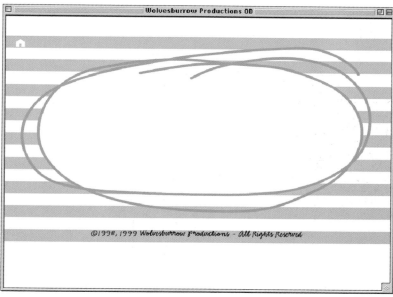

WWW.WOLVESBURROW.COM/ODCLASSIC.HTML
WOLVESBURROW PRODUCTIONS | WEBMASTER@WOLVESBURROW.COM

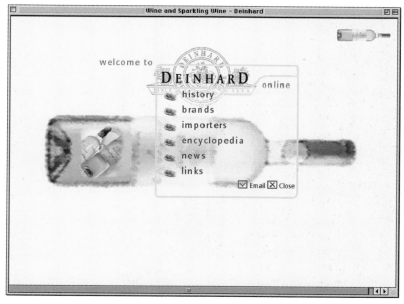

WWW.DEINHARD.COM/HTML/INDEX.SHTML
DIGITALE-ZEITEN GMBH &KAI FUNCK KOMMUNIKATIONSDESIGN & AH.WEBSOLUTIONS   GERMANY

WWW.MAX.DE/   KABEL NEW MEDIA & DIDDO RAMM, OLIVER EBERT UND THOMAS KRÜGER
MAX | WEBMASTER@ONLINE.MAX.DE   GERMANY

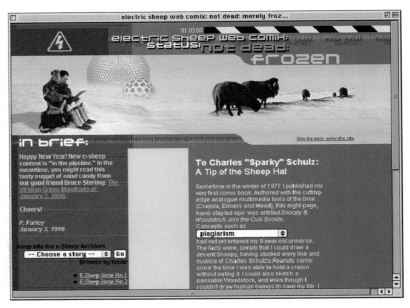

WWW.E-SHEEP.COM/
PATRICK FARLEY | PATRICK@RESORT.COM

WWW.MAKINWAVES.COM/NEW_CLIENTS/NEW_CLIENTS.HTML
SIOUXZAN PERRY | MAKIN' WAVES | SIOUXZAN@MAKINWAVES.COM   USA

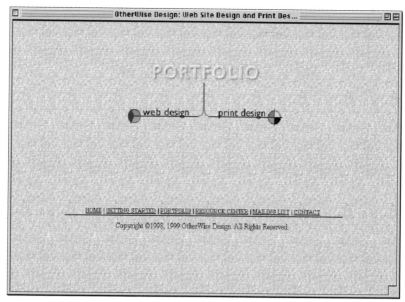

WWW.OTHERWISEDESIGN.COM/PORTFOLIO/PORTFOLIO.HTML
PETER COHEN | OTHERWISE DESIGN | INFO@OTHERWISEDESIGN.COM   USA

WWW.CLINTBAKER.COM/
CLINT BAKER | ME@CLINTBAKER.COM   USA

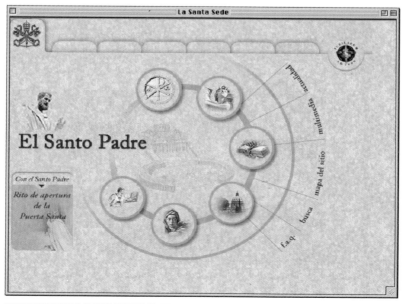

WWW.VATICAN.VA/NEWS_SERVICES/OR/HOME_ITA.HTLM
PIERO DI DOMENICANTONIO & MASSIMILIANO BRINI

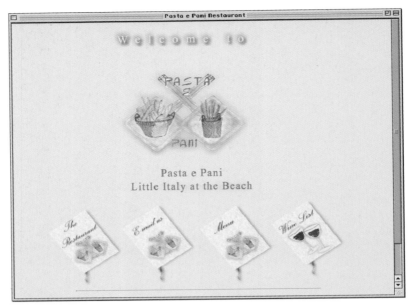

WWW.PASTA-E-PANI.COM/
MARINA CAPOBIANCO | WWW.MARXSTUDIO.COM   ITALY

WWW.WEBADDRESS.COM
DESIGNER DESIGNERMAN | DESIGN COMPANY   USA

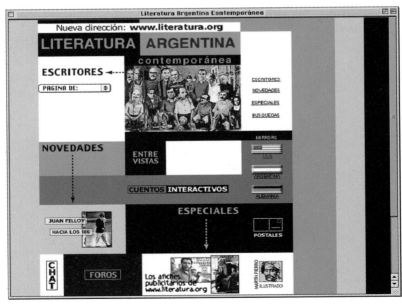

WWW.LITERATURA.ORG/
ERNESTO RESNIK | ERNESTO@LITERATURA.ORG   ARGENTINA

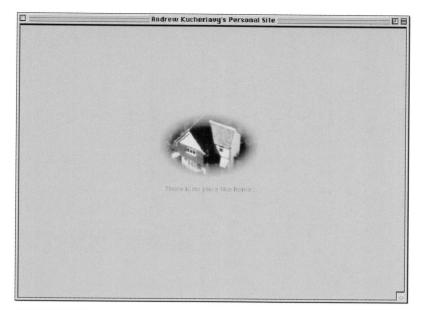

ANDREW.INTEHCNIC.COM
ANDREW A. KUCHERIAVY | INTECHNIC CORPORATION | ANDREW@INTECHNIC.COM   USA

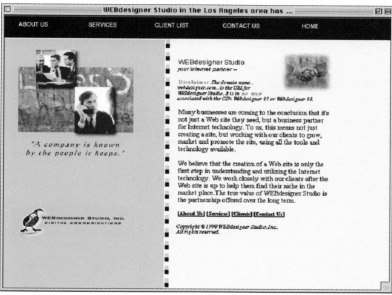

WWW.WEBDESIGNER.COM/ENTERPAGE.HTML

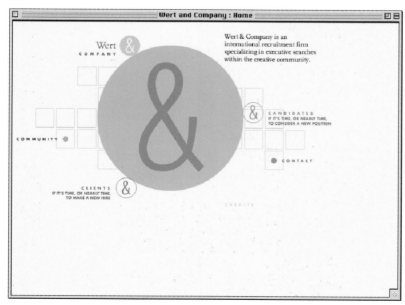

WWW.WERTCO.COM
WERT & COMPANY, INC. & I/O 360 DIGITAL DESIGN INC. | WWW.IO360.COM   USA

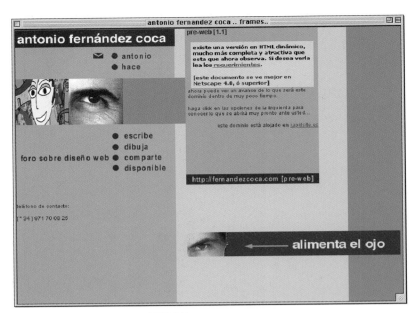

WWW.FERNANDEZCOCA.COM/WEBMATERIAL/FRAME.HTML
ANTONIO FERNÁNDEZ COCA | WWW.FERNANDEZCOCA.COM   SPAIN

WWW.WILDSTYLE.ORG
MARKUS DEUERLEIN, ROLAND KARGEL | PROJECT.INTERNETGROUP   GERMANY

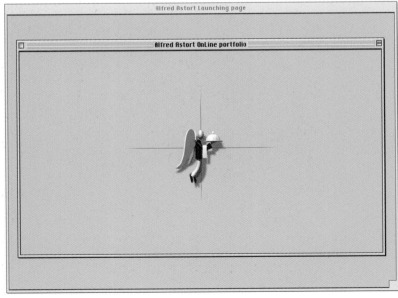

WWW.ASTORT.COM/WEB_2000/
ALFRED ASTORT | ALFRED@ASTORT.COM

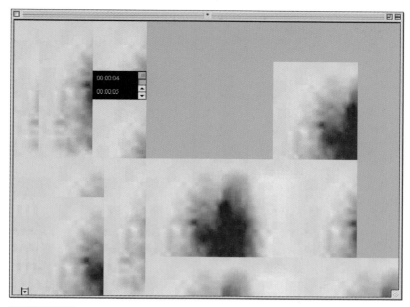

WWW.SOUPSHOP.DE/
FLORIAN THALHOFER | TH@LHOFER.COM   GERMANY

COUNTER.RAMBLER.RU/TOP100/
EGOR ARISTAKISIAN | IVAN@STACK.NET   RUSSIA

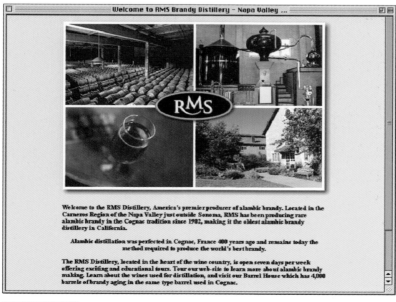

WWW.RMSBRANDY.COM/
LARRY BARNETT | BARNETT MARKETING | WWW.BARNETTMARKETING.COM   USA

WWW.BEERFOTO.COM/PEOPLE
GÜNTER BEER & FLORIAN THALHOFER | TH@LHOFER.COM　　　　　GERMANY

WWW.LUCIAS.COM/MAIN/FRAMES.HTM
MARTIN EATON | ASHANTI EATON | WWW.ASHANTIEATON.COM　　　　　USA

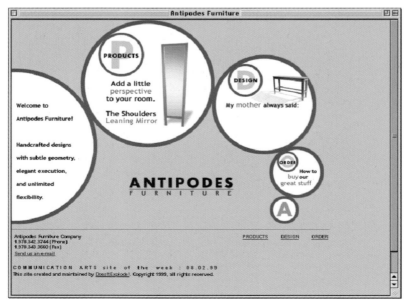

WWW.ANTIPODESFURNITURE.COM/
TODD PARKER | DOESITEXPLODE.COM | INFO@ANTIPODESFURNITURE.COM　　　　　USA

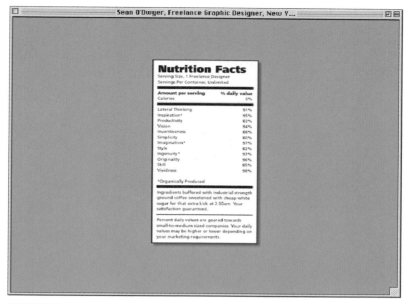

WWW.DCD.NET/
SEAN O'DWYER | DIGITAL COOKIE DESIGN | SEAN@DCD.NET USA

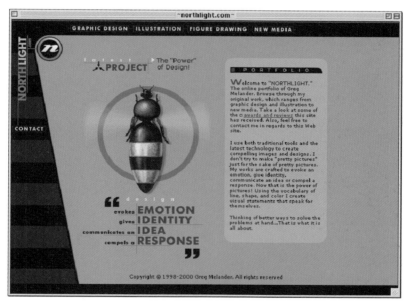

WWW.NORTHLIGHT.COM/
GREG MELANDER | GREG@NORTHLIGHT.COM USA

WWW.ARIFELDMAN.COM/
ARI FELDMAN | ARI@ARIFELDMAN.COM USA

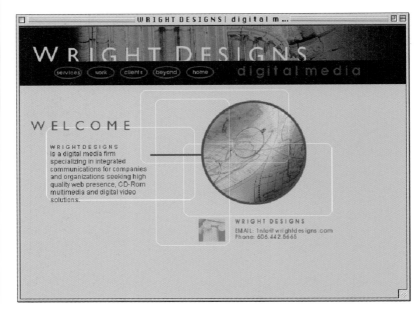

WWW.WRIGHTDESIGNS.COM/
RANDALL WRIGHT | WRIGHT DESIGNS

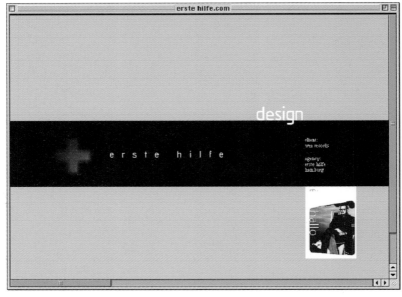

WWW.ERSTEHILFE.COM/DESIGN.HTM

WWW.SHIFT.JP.ORG/
NOFRONTIERE | SHIFT@JP.ORG   JAPAN

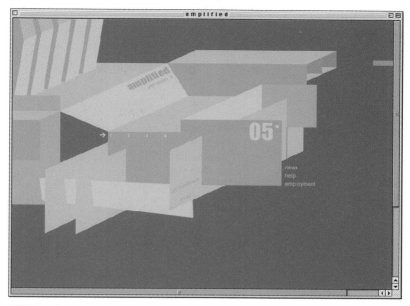

AMPLIFIED.NU/AMPLIFIED/VERSION5/INDEX.HTML
MICHAEL CHENG | AMPLIFIED@AMPLIFIED.NU

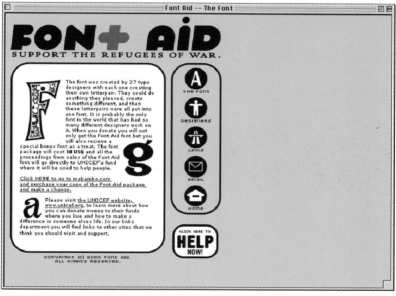

WWW.FUELFONTS.COM/FONTAID/FONT.HTML

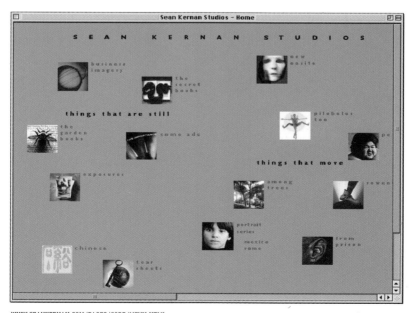

WWW.SEANKERNAN.COM/PAGES/CORE/MENU.HTML
MATTHEW GARRETT | SEAN KERNAN   USA

171

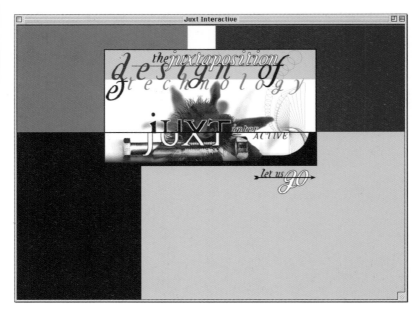

WWW.JUXTINTERACTIVE.COM
STEVE WAGES, TODD PURGASON, LUIS ESCOREAL, JOSH FORSTOT | INFO@JUXTINTERACTIVE.COM   USA

WWW.ABARGON.COM/ABARGON/HOME/HOME.HTML
JORGE HERRERA, JUAN CARLOS ARIAS | ABARGON | INFO@ABARGON.COM

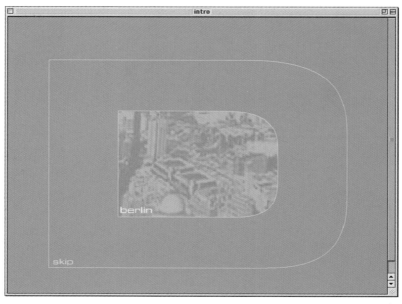

CLAUDIA-STEIN-DESIGN.COM/INTRO.HTML
CLAUDIA STEIN DESIGN | INFO@CLAUDIA-STEIN-DESIGN.COM   GERMANY

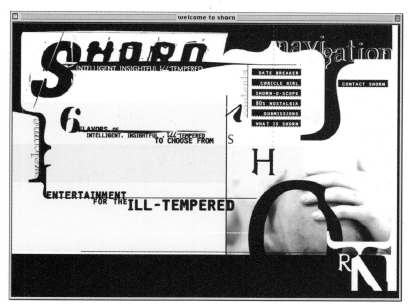

WWW.SHORN.COM/INDEX2.HTML
TODD PURGASON | JUXTINTERACTIVE | WWW.JUXTINTERACTIVE.COM

USA

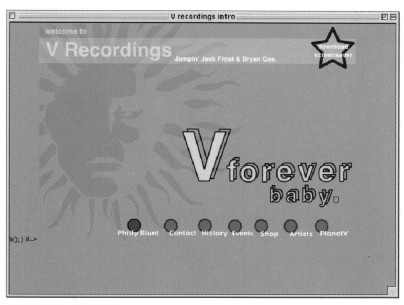

WWW.VRECORDINGS.COM/INTRO.HTM

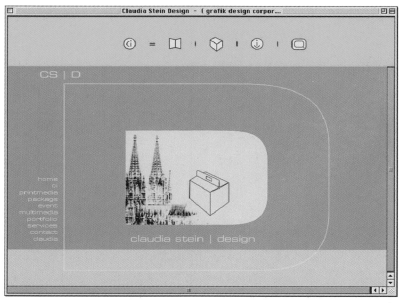

CLAUDIA-STEIN-DESIGN.COM/START.HTML
CLAUDIA STEIN DESIGN | INFO@CLAUDIA-STEIN-DESIGN.COM

GERMANY

WWW.BITTERWAITRESS.COM/
CHRISTOPHER FEHLINGER

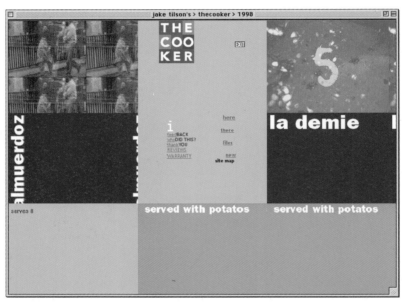

WWW.THECOOKER.COM/
JAKE TILSON | ©ATLAS 1994-2000 | JAKE@THECOOKER.COM   USA

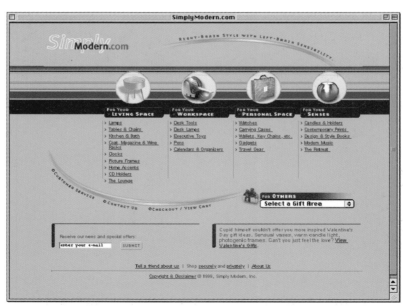

WWW.SIMPLYMODERN.COM/SCRIPTS/INDEX.CFM
JON RITTENBERG ,JASON PRINCE |SIMPLY MODERN, INC. | JASON@SIMPLYMODERN.COM   USA

WWW.BURTON.CO.JP/CORE/
DAVE BUCKLAND, CHUCK WHITE | BURTON | INFO@BURTON.COM   USA

WWW.WEB-DESIGN.CO.IL/
WEBPROM DESIGN | WWW.WEB-DESIGN.CO.IL   ISRAEL

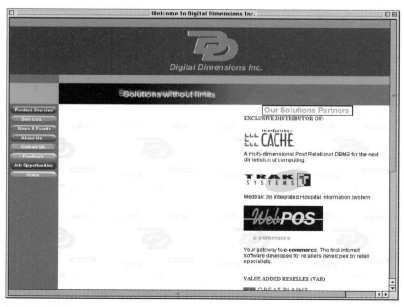

WWW.DDI.COM.PH/
GRACIOUS@IS.COM.PH   PHILIPPINES

WWW.MESSYGOURMET.COM/
INFO@MESSYGOURMET.COM

USA

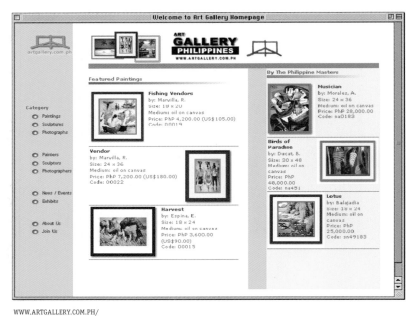

WWW.ARTGALLERY.COM.PH/
MELROSE ANG, BALLYHOO INTERNATIONAL SERVICES | MEL@BALLYNET.COM

PHILIPPINES

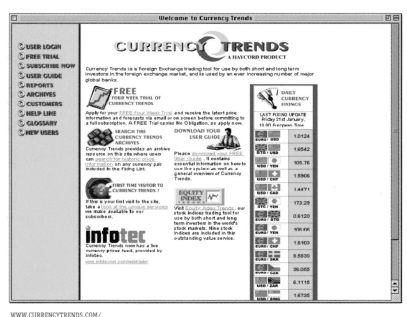

WWW.CURRENCYTRENDS.COM/
DREAMTEAM | INFO@DREAMTEAM.CO.UK

UK

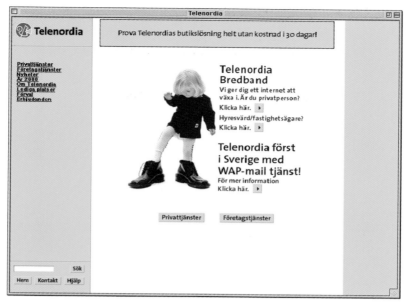

WWW.TELENORDIA.SE/

SWEDEN

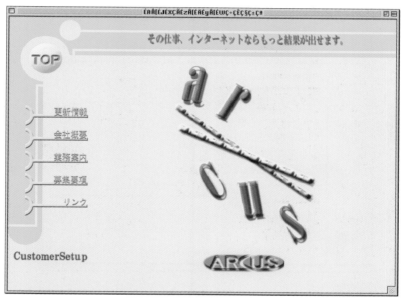

WWW.ARCUS.CO.JP/

JAPAN

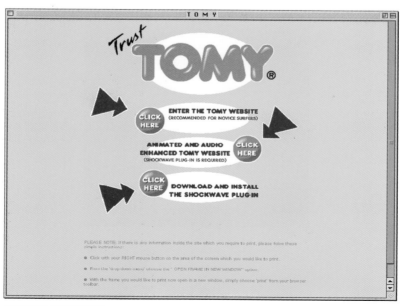

WWW.TOMY.CO.UK/INDEXIE.HTM

WWW.INSOMNIOUS.COM | NOSLEEP@INSOMNIOUS.COM

UK

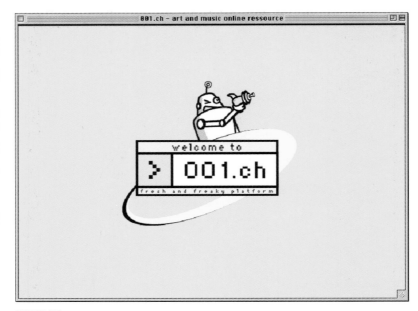

WWW.001.CH/
NOTHING MEDIALAB | WWW.NOTHING.CH   SWITZERLAND

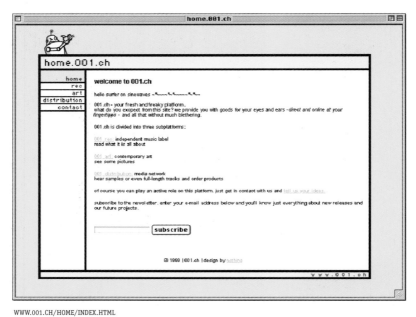

WWW.001.CH/HOME/INDEX.HTML
NOTHING MEDIALAB | WWW.NOTHING.CH   SWITZERLAND

WWW.THESTREAM.COM/CH/HTML/LANDING/YAHOOCHINESE.HTML

                                                                    USA

WWW.AMBEROL.CO.UK/INDEX.HTM

UK

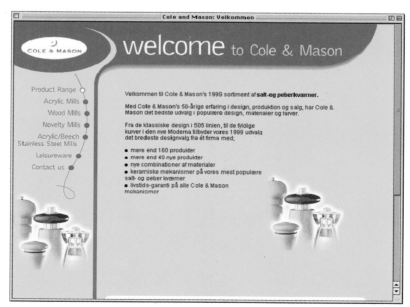

WWW.CYCLEIRELAND.COM/START.HTM
SEAN@DCD.NET

WWW.COLEANDMASON.CO.UK/WELCOMEDK.HTM
WHITELIGHT DESIGN & PETER COOPER

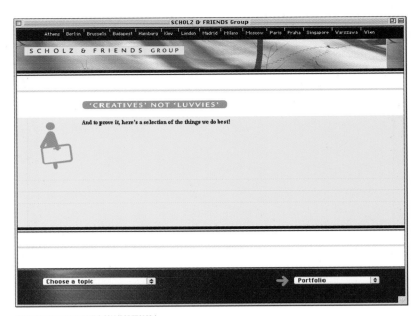

WWW.SCHOLZ-AND-FRIENDS.COM/PORTFOLIO/
N.A.S.A. 2.0 | WWW.NASA20.COM   GERMANY

KITPROD.HYPERMART.NET/LOGIN/INDEX2.HTML
POOIKIT@TM.NET.MY   MALAYSIA

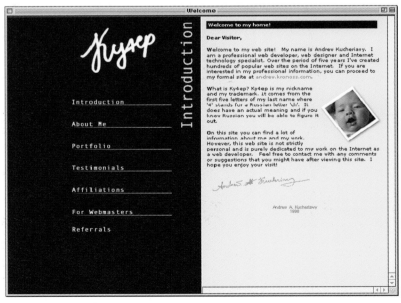

KY4EP.KRONOSS.COM/
ANDREW A. KUCHERIAVY | INTECHNIC CORPORATION | ANDREW@INTECHNIC.COM   USA

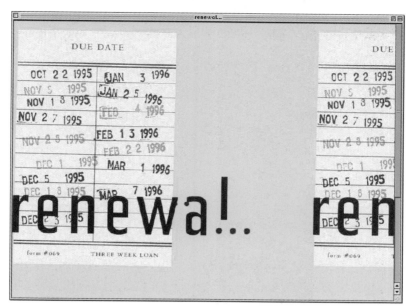

FOUNDATIONFLUX.COM/NLBFORUM/
ADRIAN AND JIMMY FOR ETC/WOOFERXP PRODUCTION © | INPUT@FOUNDATIONFLUX.COM

HOME4U.HONGKONG.COM/MONEY/CAREER/ESWORK/

HONG KONG

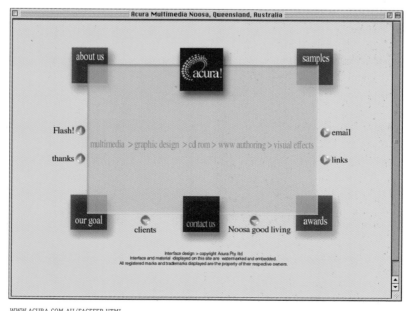

WWW.ACURA.COM.AU/FACEFEB.HTML
JEAN-PAUL PALLANDRE, ACURA MULTIMEDIA PTY LTD | JEANPAUL@HOTKEY.NET.AU   AUSTRALIA

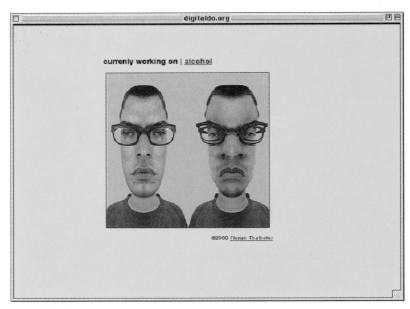

currently working on | alcohol

©2000 Florian Thalhofer

WWW.DIGITALDO.ORG
FLORIAN THALHOFER | TH@ALHOFER.COM   GERMANY

WWW.E4ME.COM/FPC/FPC.HTML
RAZORFISH   USA

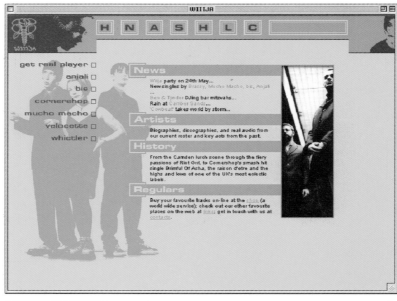

WWW.WINONA-DOT.COM/WIIIJA/
JOE NAVIN | WINONA-DOT.COM | WWW.WINONA-DOT.COM   UK

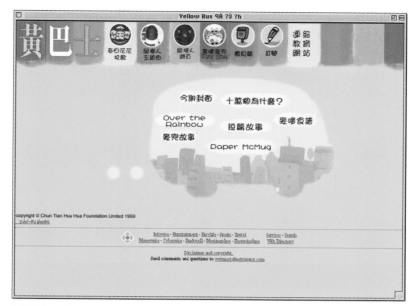

WWW2.NETVIGATOR.COM/ENTE/YBUS/INDEX.HTML

CHINA

WWW.SCHOEPFER.DE/

GERMANY

WWW.SCHOEPFER.DE/FRAMESET.HTM

GERMANY

WWW.FOCUS-ONLINE.COM/

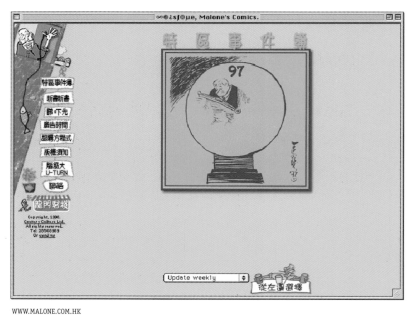

WWW.MALONE.COM.HK
DIGITALONE LTD. | INFO@MALONE.COM.HK   HONG KONG

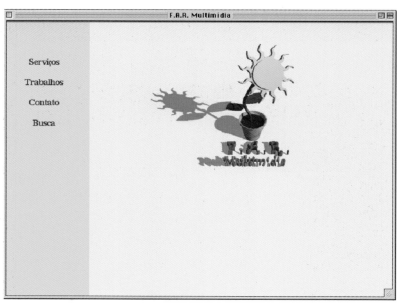

MEMBERS.AOL.COM/FARMULTIMIDIA/FRAME.HTML

                                                        BRAZIL

WWW.TIPP24.DE

GERMANY

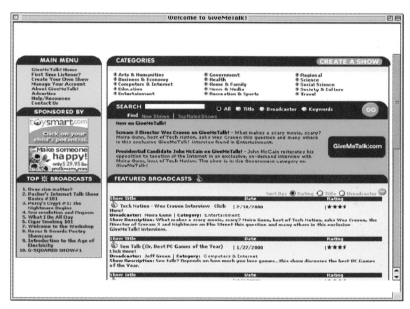

WWW.GIVEMETALK.COM/
DAVID EPSTEIN VP, PRODUCT DEVELOPMENT

WWW.BREAKFASTBOYS.COM/PRANGER.HTM
STEPHEN OACHS | PIXELMATION INTERNET TECHNOLOGIES | STEPHEN@PIXELMATION.COM   USA

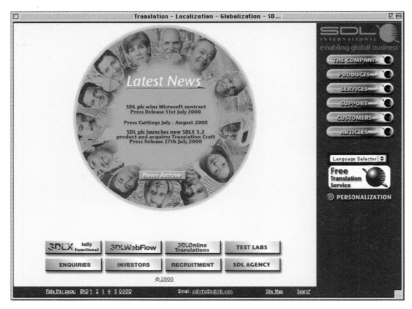

WWW.SDLINTL.COM/FRAMEHTM/MAIN.H
PHILIP NICHOLS | SDL INTERNATIONAL | WEBMASTER@SDLINTL.COM   UK

WWW.TIMBERNET.CO.IL/
WEBPROM DESIGN | WWW.WEB-DESIGN.CO.IL   ISRAEL

WWW.MEANINGGREEN.SE/MG.HTML   TONE KNIBESTÖL, EMIL TAVASSOLI, PIJASUNDIN
SATAMA INTERACTIVE | WWW.SATAMA.COM   SWEDEN

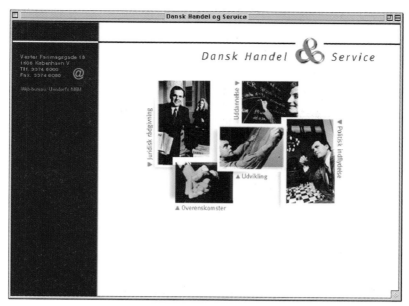

WWW.DHS.DK/
ULENDORF'S M&M | INFO@ULENDORF.DK   DENMARK

WWW.WENXUE.COM/B5/
XIANG ZI | OLIVE TREE LITERATURE SOCIETY | WEBMASTER@WENXUE.COM

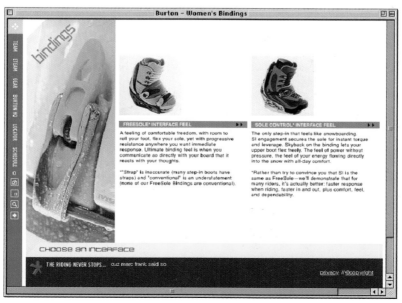

WWW.BURTON.COM/
DAVE BUCKLAND, CHUCK WHITE | BURTON | INFO@BURTON.COM   USA

WWW.FRAMFAB.DK
JONAS LINELL, CHRISTIAN ZANDER | FRAMFAB.DK | DENMARK   DENMARK

WWW.POESIA.COM/
EMILIANO PEREZ PENA | WS ARGENTINA   ARGENTINA

WWW.ALTREC.COM/
COREY KAISER | WWW.ALTREC.COM   KEVYN SMITH, ENOCH PLATAS, ELENA MOON,
USA

WWW.PARISHAIR.CJB.NET
DOM MURPHY | TAK!TAK! | WWW.TAKTAK.CO.UK UK

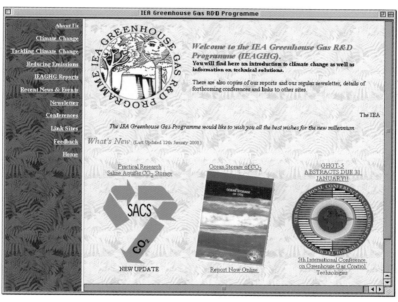

WWW.IEAGREEN.ORG.UK/
ANDREA SMITH UK

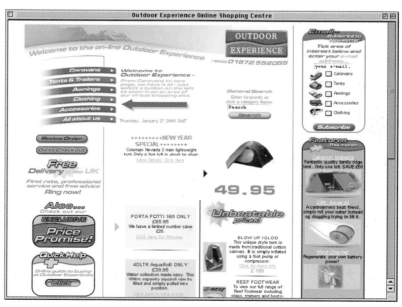

WWW.OUTDOOREXPERIENCE.CO.UK/
WEB SIGHT LTD | WWW.WEB-SIGHT.CO.UK UK

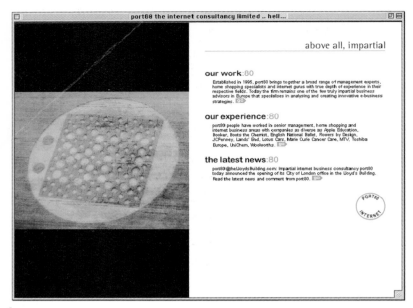

WWW.PORT80.CO.UK/

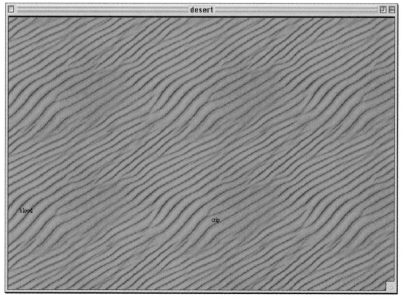

WWW.CYNTHIAMYERS.COM/MENU/MENU.HTML SIOUXZAN PERRY, WEBMISTRESS EXTRAORDINAIRE |
WWW.MAKINWAVES.COM   USA

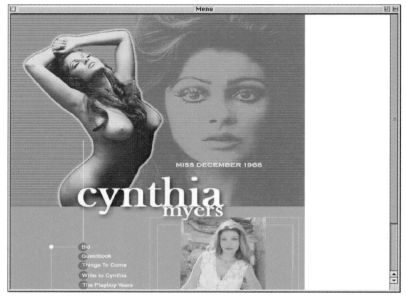

WWW.BLOODS.COM/HIDEOUT/
DIRKSTER PRODUCTIONS

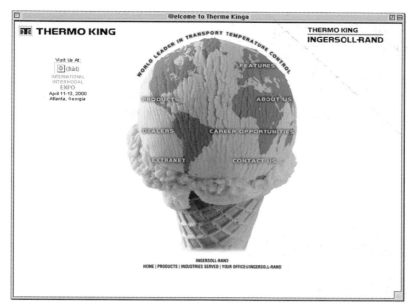

WWW.THERMOKING.COM/

USA

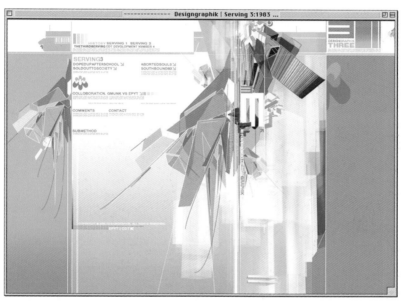

WWW.DESIGNGRAPHIK.COM/
MIKE YOUNG | EPYT | MIKE@DESIGNGRAPHIK.COM

WWW.PIXELMASSAKER.COM/
BETTY MASSKAKER | BETTY@PIXELMASSAKER.COM

WWW.MOVIESOUNDS.COM/

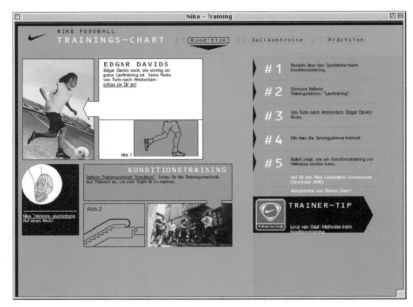

WWW.NIKE.COM/FEATURES/
OLAF CZESCHNER | NEUE DIGITALE | WWW.NEUE-DIGITALE.DE

GERMANY

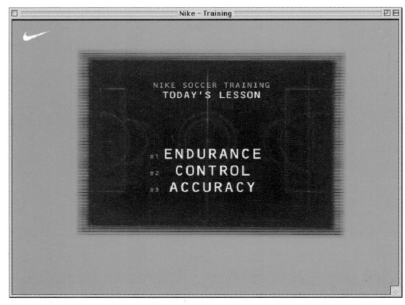

WWW.NIKE.COM/FEATURES/90_MINUTES/START.HTML
OLAF CZESCHNER | NEUE DIGITALE | WWW.NEUE-DIGITALE.DE

GERMANY

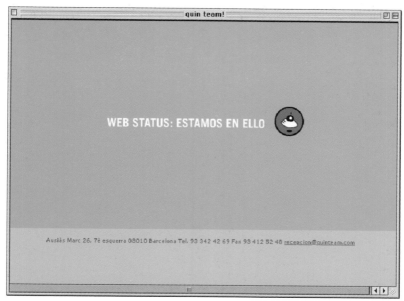

WWW.QUINTEAM.COM
JAUME PERIS, ORIOL GRANES, BRUNO BARRACHINA | QUIN TEAM!

SPAIN

SZE.BITLOUNGE.COM/
GOH SZE YING | S_ZYNC@USA.NET

MALAYSIA

WWW.JAQUEMATECOM.COM/BOOK2.HTM
JUAN CARLOS CAMAERT | WWW.CAMMAERT.COM

SPAIN

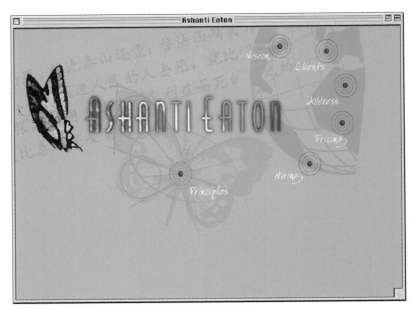

WWW.ASHANTIEATON.COM/MAIN.HTM
BEN MCCOY | ASHANTI EATON | WWW.ASHANTIEATON.COM   USA

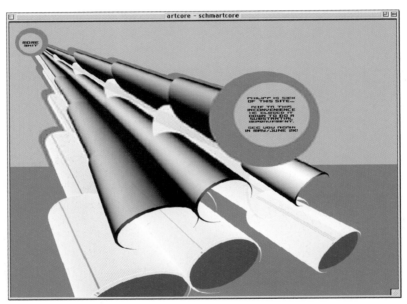

WWW.PUK.DE/ARTCORE/FRAMESET.HTML
PHILIPP KOERBER | MEDIADESIGNTASKFORCE | ARTCORE@PUK.DE   GERMANY

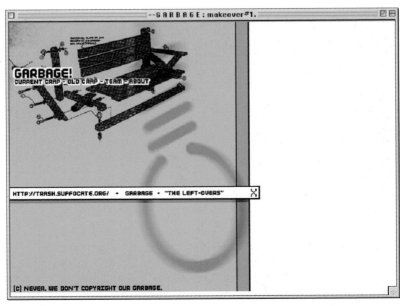

WWW.SUFFOCATE.ORG/
CEDRIC DEWULF | WWW.C3DRIC.COM/

WWW.EYE4U.COM/
EYE4U ACTIVE MEDIA | TM@EYE4U.COM

GERMANY

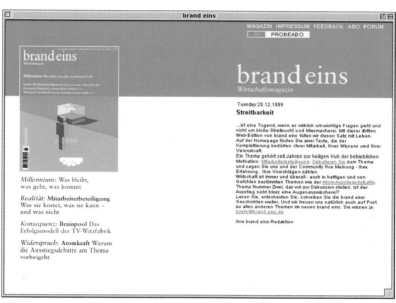

WWW.BRANDEINS.COM/HOME.PHP
MATTHIAS BALLMANN | MATTHIAS@BALLMANN.NET

GERMANY

WWW.RTHK.ORG.HK/RTHK/MD/MD9802/FEB_FRONT.HTML

HONG KONG

WWW.ELPAIS.ES/
SANTIAGO CARBAJO | EL PAIS DIGITAL   SPAIN

WWW.BRADLEYJPARRISH.COM/JAVAHOME.HTML
BRADLEY J. PARRISH   USA

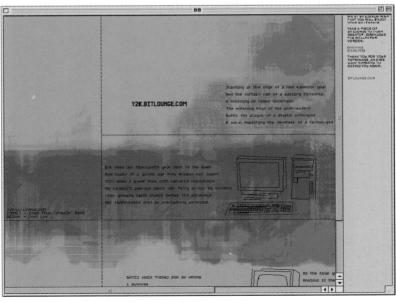

Y2K.BITLOUNGE.COM/
JOSHUA LIM TSENG CHUAN

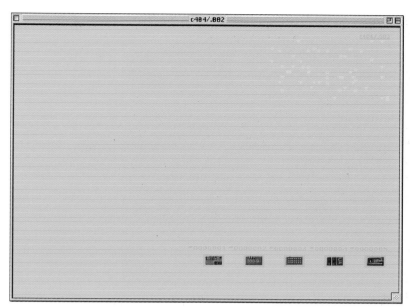

WWW.C404.COM/

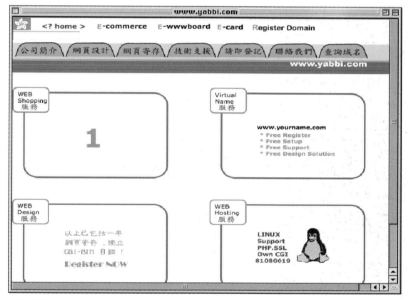

WWW.YABBI.COM/

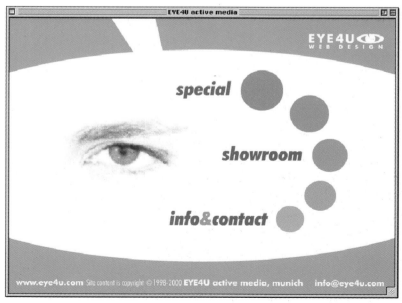

WWW.EYE4U.COM/HOME/INDEX.HTM
EYE4U ACTIVE MEDIA | TM@EYE4U.COM

GERMANY

WWW.BIGDIG.COM/

USA

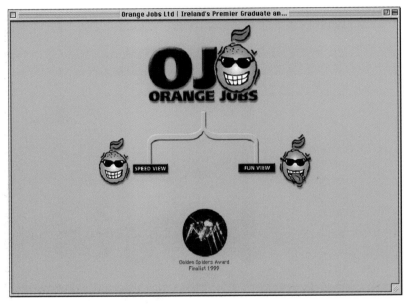

WWW.ORANGEJOBS.COM/
INFO@ORANGEJOBS.COM

UK

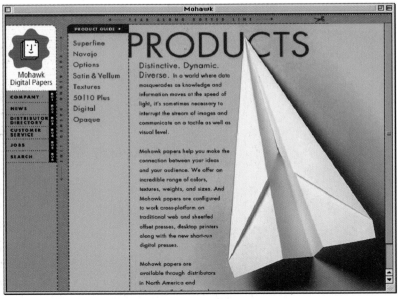

WWW.MOHAWKPAPER.COM/PRODUCTS/INDEX.EHTML

USA

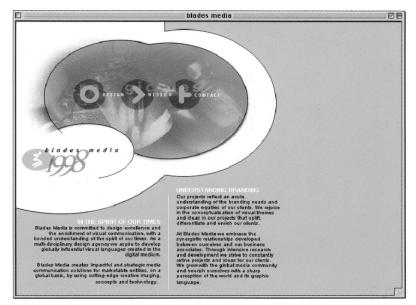

WWW.BLADES.CO.ZA/CONTENTS.HTM
MEDIA@BLADES.CO.ZA   SOUTH AFRICA

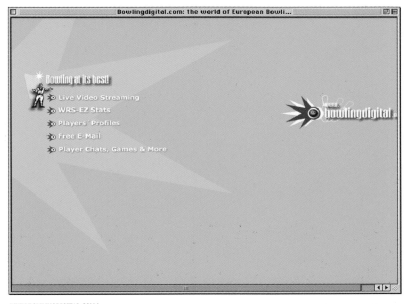

WWW.BOWLINGDIGITAL.COM/
KABEL NEW MEDIA GMBH | WWW.KABEL.DE   GERMANY

WWW.LIVELY-ARTS.CO.UK/
TREVOR@LIVELY-ARTS.CO.UK   UK

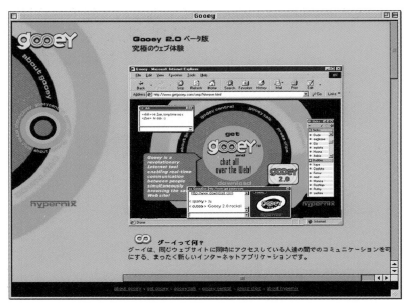

WWW.GOOEY.COM/CMP/ABOUT.ASP?LANG=JP

WWW.PRIMEART.NET/
OZGUR OZTURK, ERSIN BASARAN | PRIMEART WEBGROUP | INFO@PRIMEART.NET   TURKEY

WWW.JAPANSOCKS.DE/
MARKUS ROTH | ROTH@ODN.DE   GERMANY

212

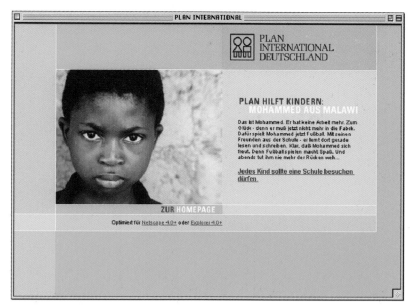

WWW.PLAN-INTERNATIONAL.DE/
N.A.S.A.2.0 GMBH | WWW.NASA20.COM   GERMANY

WWW.REDBEAN.COM/

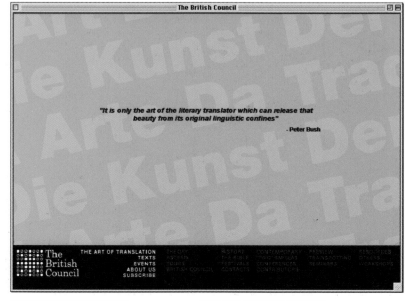

WWW.LITERARYTRANSLATION.COM/IN   SIMON CRAB, DAVID JONES, SAM COLLET,
SIARON HUGHES | LATERAL NET LTD. | WWW.LATERAL.NET   UK

WWW.EGOMEDIA.COM/EGO2000MAIN.HTM
EGO MEDIA USA

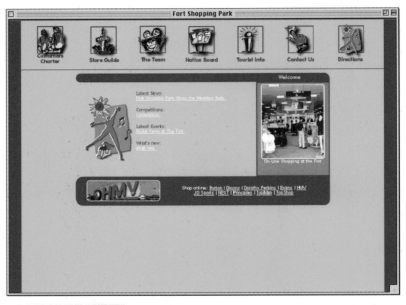

WWW.THEFORT.CO.UK/FRAMESET.HTML
ED RICHARDSON, LISA KENNEDY, JERRY WERRETT | NETWORKS | WWW.NETWORKS.CO.UK UK

WWW.LIVELY-ARTS.CO.UK/INTRO.HTM
TREVOR@LIVELY-ARTS.CO.UK UK

WWW.FORKINHAND.COM/BIGD/BIGD.HTM

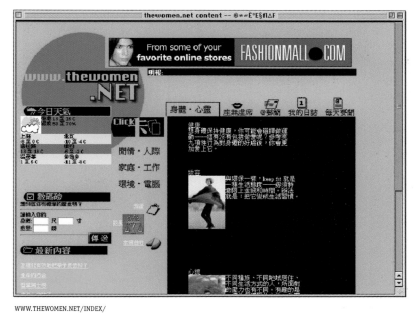

WWW.THEWOMEN.NET/INDEX/
SUNVALLEY COMMUNICATIONS   HONG KONG

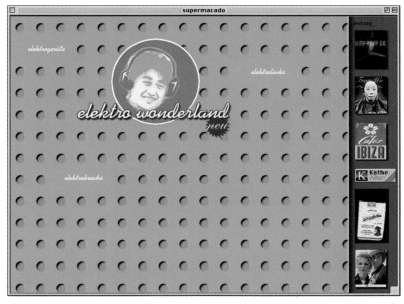

WWW.E-7.COM/~VIETS/SUPERMARKT   PAUL APOSTOLOU, OLIVER VIETS
ELEPHANT SEVEN GMBH | E-7.COM   GERMANY

WWW.PLANETRAPIDO.COM

UK

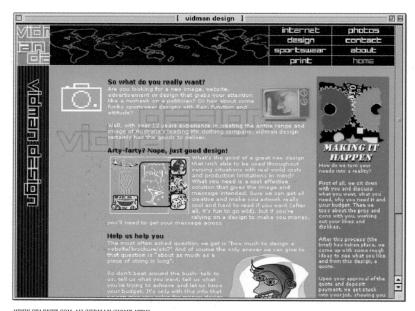

WWW.STARNET.COM.AU/VIDMAN/HOME.HTML
DAVID RAFFERTON | VIDMAN DESIGN | VIDMAN@STARNET.COM.AU

AUSTRALIA

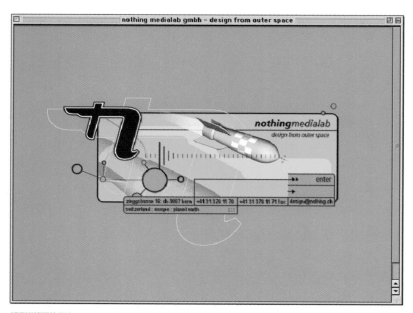

WWW.NOTHING.CH/
BASTIAAN VAN ROODEN | NOTHING MEDIALAB GMBH | DESIGN@NOTHING.CH

SWITZERLAND

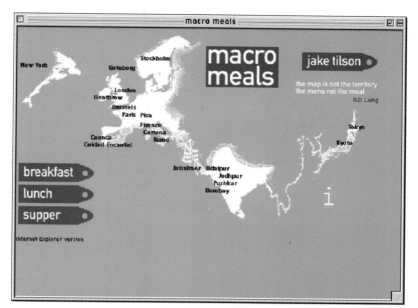

WWW.THECOOKER.COM/HERE/MACRO/MEALS.HTML
JAKE TILSON | ©ATLAS 1994-2000 | JAKE@THECOOKER.COM

USA

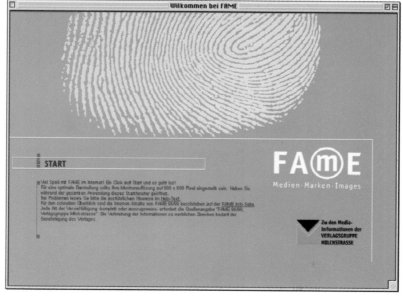

WWW.BOO.COM/

WWW.FAME-IMAGES.DE/START/DE/HTML/INDEX.HTML

GERMANY

WWW.SAPIENT.COM
SAPIENT | INFO@SAPIENT.COM

USA

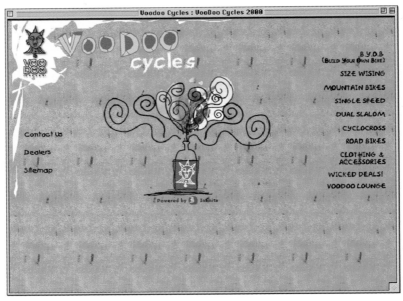

WWW.VOODOO-CYCLES.COM/

WWW.BADBOYONLINE.COM/FRAMESET
KIOKEN INCORPORATED | WWW.KIOKEN.COM

USA

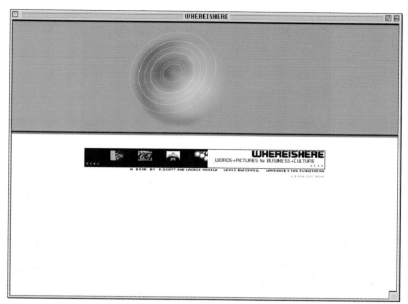

WWW.WHEREISHERE.COM/WHEREISHERE/INDEX.HTML

WWW.THECOOKER.COM/HERE/SOFT/SIGN.HTML
JAKE TILSON | ©ATLAS 1994-2000 | JAKE@THECOOKER.COM   USA

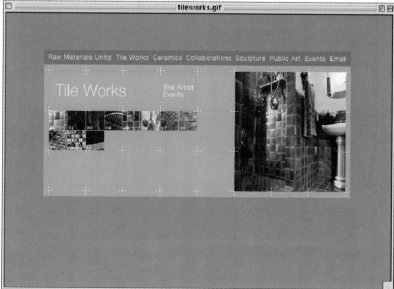

WWW.RAWMATERIALSUNLTD.COM/TILEWORKS.HTM

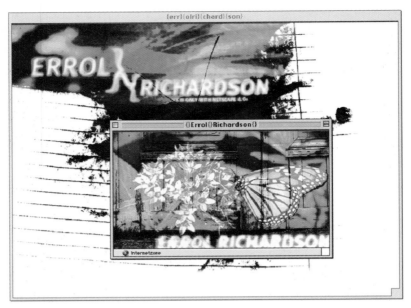

WWW.ERROLRICHARDSON.COM
ERROL RICHARDSON   UK

WWW.FORK.DE/V3.3/PROJECT
FORK UNSTABLE MEDIA | INFO@FORK.DE   GERMANY

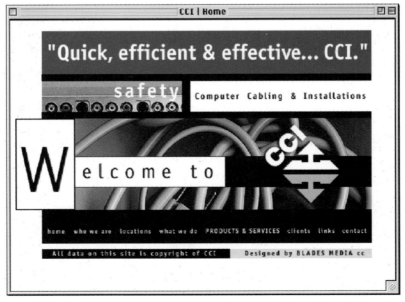

WWW.CCI.CO.ZA/CONTENTS.HTML
BLADES | WWW.BLADES.CO.ZA   SOUTH AFRICA

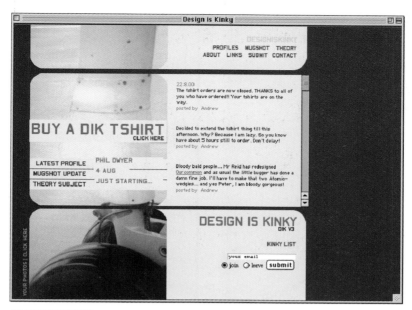

WWW.DESIGNISKINKY.NET/
ANDREW JOHNSTONE | INFO@DESIGNISKINKY.NET

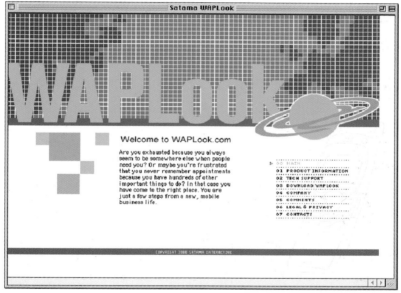

WWW.WAPLOOK.COM
JAKOB SWEDENBORG ET AL | SATAMA INTERACTIVE | WWW.SATAMA.COM   SWEDEN

WWW.CITRUSDESIGN.NU/FOREFATHERS/HTML/FLIGHT.HTM
ROBB THOMPSON, STEPHEN SEELEY | ROBB@CITRUSDESIGN.NU

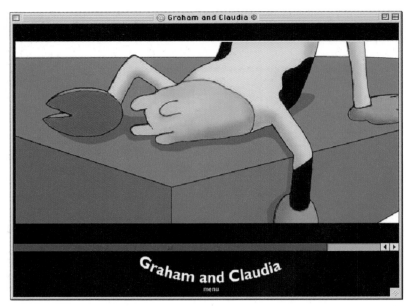

WWW.GRAHAMANDCLAUDIA.COM/GANDC.HTM   SIMON CRAB, DAVID JONES, SAM COLLET
SIARON HUGHES | LATERAL NET LTD. | WWW.LATERAL.NET   UK

WWW.GOERTZ-SCHUHE.DE/INDEX2.HTML
ANDREAS FEY | SINNERSCHRADER.DE   GERMANY

WWW.KANGLEE.COM/INDEX1.HTML
KIOKEN INCORPORATED | WWW.KIOKEN.COM   USA

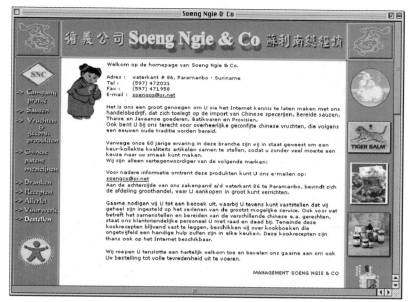

WWW.SOENGNGIE.SR/
ROBERT VOIGT | WEB CREATORS SURINAME N.V. | WWW.WEBCREATORS.SR   SURINAM

WWW.DALER-ROWNEY.CO.UK/IE/DEFAULT.HTML
BRAINSTORMERS WEB FACTORY & TRACY MASON | DALER-ROWNEY LTD   UK

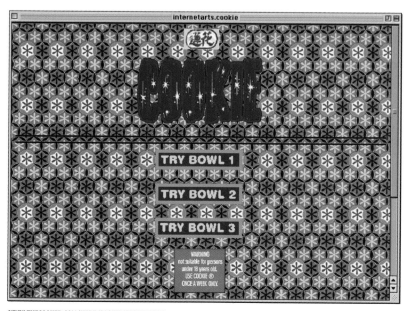

WWW.THECOOKER.COM/HERE/COOKIE/COOKIE.HTML
JAKE TILSON | ©ATLAS 1994-2000 | JAKE@THECOOKER.COM   USA

WWW.MADASAFISH.COM/
INFO@MADASAFISH.COM

WWW.PAULSMITH.CO.UK/DEFINITIVE/
FORESIGHT (EUROPE) LTD. | WWW.FORESIGHT.CO.UK

UK

WWW.HACKERSCANYON.COM/CANYONDR.HTM

WWW.HEADWAYINST.COM/
SIXTYEIGHT CREATIVE SOLUTIONS | SOLUTIONS@SIXTYEIGHT.CO.UK   UK

WWW.HUTCHCITY.COM/
FREDDY CHEUNG, MARCUS NG | WEBMASTER@HUTCHCITY.COM   HONG KONG

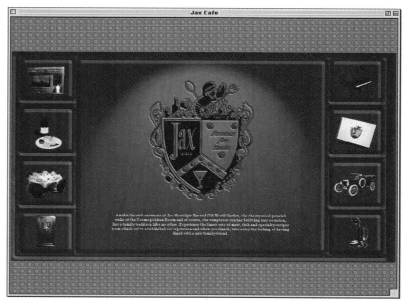

WWW.JAXCAFE.COM/MAIN/FRAMES.HTM
TERI FIRKINS | ASHANTI EATON | WWW.ASHANTIEATON.COM   USA

WWW.CONFUSED.CO.UK/VIRGIN/MAIN.HTML
SALLY COE | FOLD7 | EMMA@CONFUSED.CO.UK   UK

WWW.CERAMASPEED.COM/
10 GROUP PLC | WWW.10GROUP.CO.UK   UK

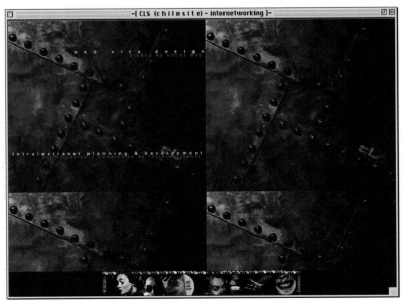

WWW.CHILESITE.COM/HOME.HTM
CLS CHILESITE | INFO@CHILESITE.COM   CHILE

WWW.CONFASHION.COM/
SAWETZ.COM | KARIN@SAWETZ.COM

AUSTRIA

WWW.BUCSSTORE.COM/
DIGISCRIBE | WWW.DIGISCRIBE.COM

WWW.KAZZ107.COM/
PIXELMATION INTERNET TECHNOLOGIES | WWW.PIXELMATION.COM

STEPHEN OACHS, JUSTIN KELLEY
USA

WWW.PEARLRIVER.COM/DEPARTMENT.HTML
GLASS PLANET INDUSTRIES | WWW.GLASSPLANET.COM   UK

WWW.RIGBYANDPELLER.COM/
DOMINO SYSTEMS | WWW.DOMINO.COM   UK

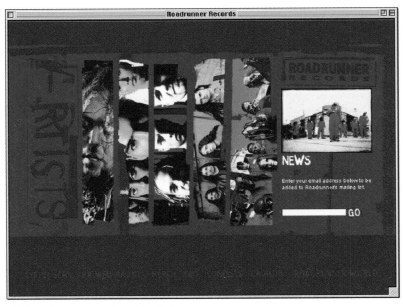

WWW.ROADRUNNERRECORDS.COM/ROADRUNNER.HTML
DEEP CREATIVE LTD. | WWW.DEEP.CO.UK   UK

WWW.SF.SE/FORETAGSBILJETTER/
SF BIO AB | WEBMASTER@SF.SE   SWEDEN

WWW.SLEAZENATION.COM/
GARETH JENKINS, DARRYL HARDMAN, MARTIN HOLLYWOOD | SWINSTEAD PUBLISHING   UK

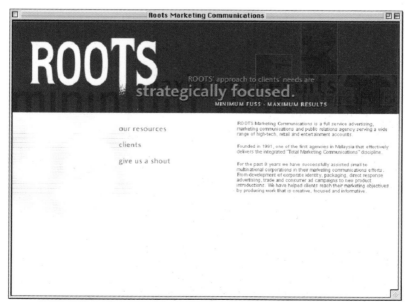

WWW.ROOTS.COM.MY
ANDY LIM | ANDY@ARTDIRECTORS.COM   MALAYSIA

WWW.FRUEH.DE/
THOMAS DINGER | COMPUTERZEIT OHG | WWW.COMPUTERZEIT.DE   GERMANY

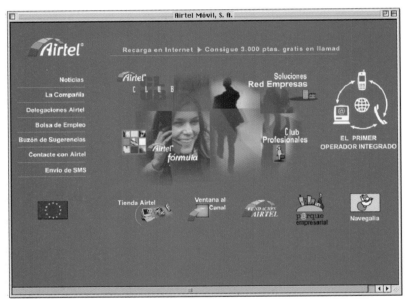

WWW.FRUEH.DE/
THOMAS DINGER | COMPUTERZEIT OHG | WWW.COMPUTERZEIT.DE   GERMANY

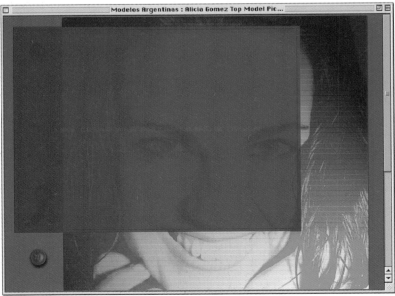

WWW.ALICIAGOMEZ.COM.AR/BEGIN.HTM
MIKE CESAR, ALICIA GOMEZ | ALICIA@MODELOSWEB.COM   ARGENTINA

WWW.AROS.DK/
ÖRN ÓLASON | ADERA+ | ORN.OLASON@ADERAGROUP.COM   DENMARK

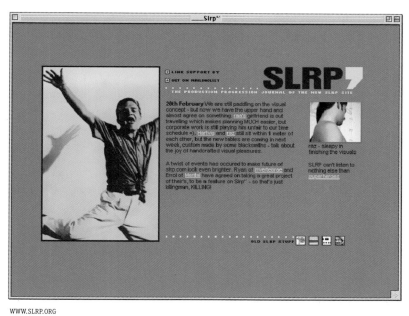

WWW.SLRP.ORG
SLRP | NICO@SLRP.CO   DENMARK

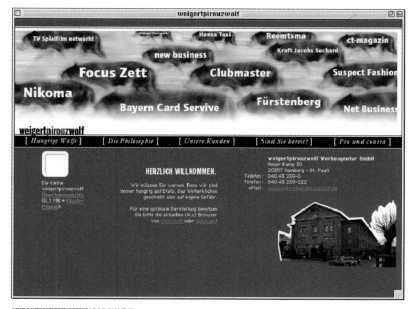

WWW.WEIGERTPIROUZWOLF.DE/HOME.H
WEIGERTPIROUZWOLF & N.A.S.A.2.0 GMBH | WWW.NASA20.DE   GERMANY

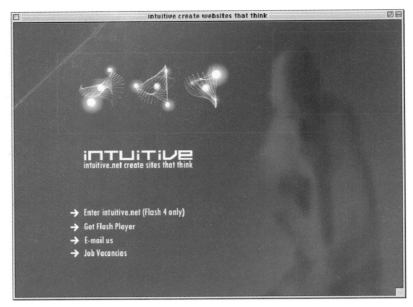

WWW.INTUITIVENET.CO.UK

UK

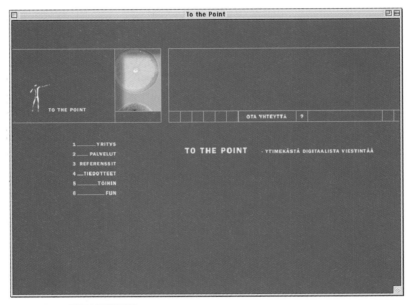

WWW.TOTHEPOINT.FI/HTML/INDEX.HTML

FINLAND

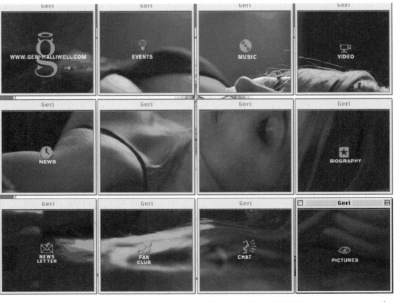

WWW.GERI-HALLIWELL.COM
LATERAL NET LTD. | WWW.LATERAL.NET

SIMON CRAB, DAVID JONES, SAM COLLET,SIARON HUGHES

UK

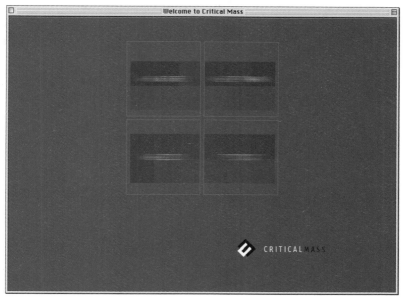

WWW.CRITICALMASS.COM/CONTENT_FS.HTML
RANDALL S. WILLCOX | CRITICAL MASS INC. | WEBMASTER@CRITICALMASS.AB.CA   USA

WWW.LAURENT-PERRIER.DE/   DIGITALE-ZEITEN GMBH
& K AI FUNCK KOMMUNIKATIONSDESIGN & AH.WEBSOLUTIONS   GERMANY

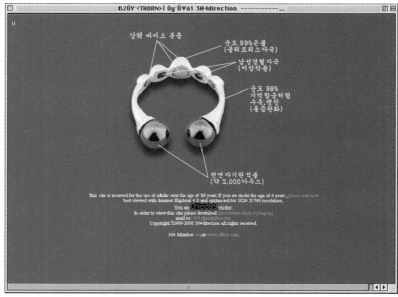

WWW.304.CO.KR/

                                                                KOREA

CNY.BITLOUNGE.COM/
JOSHUA LIM TSENG CHUAN | JL@BITLOUNGE.COM

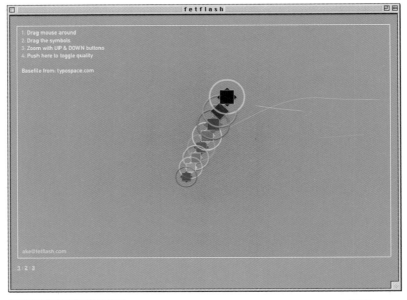

WWW.FETFLASH.COM/INDEX_02.HTML
ÅKE BRATTBERG | WWW.FAMESTUDIOS.SE

SWEDEN

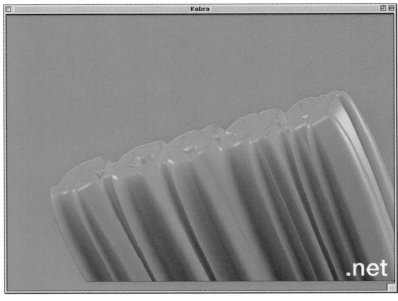

WWW.KOBRA.NET/INDEX_IE.HTML
MAGNUS HÖGGREN | MAGNUS@KOBRA.NET

WWW.ONEOFAKIND.COM.AU/FLASHED.HTML
ONE OF A KIND MEDIA GROUP PTY. LTD. | DESIGN@ONEOFAKIND.COM.AU

KATIE M. LITTLE
AUSTRALIA

WWW.LEVI.COM/SPRING/NONFLASHED.HTML
ROGER WONG | MARCH FIRST

USA

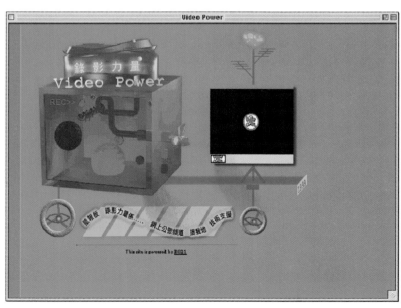

WWW.VIDEOPOWER.ORG.HK/
DIGITALONE LTD. | WWW.DG21.COM

HONG KONG

WWW.BARNEYS.COM/ENTER.HTML
KIOKEN INCORPORATED | WWW.KIOKEN.COM

USA

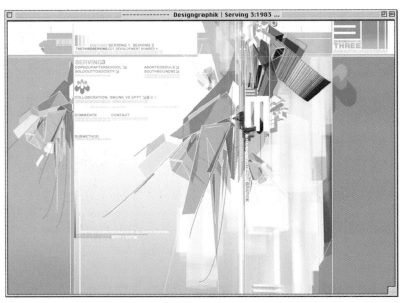

WWW.DESIGNGRAPHIK.COM/
MIKE YOUNG | EPYT | MIKE@DESIGNGRAPHIK.COM

WWW.EGREETINGS.COM/E-PRODUCTS/M_MAIN/CGI/HOMEPAGE

USA

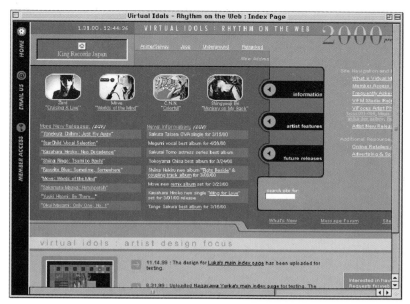

V-IDOLS.SIMPLENET.COM/

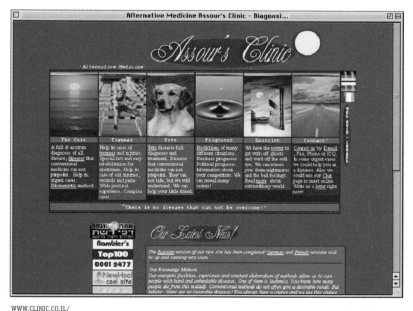

WWW.CLINIC.CO.IL/
WEBPROM DESIGN | WWW.WEB-DESIGN.CO.IL   ISRAEL

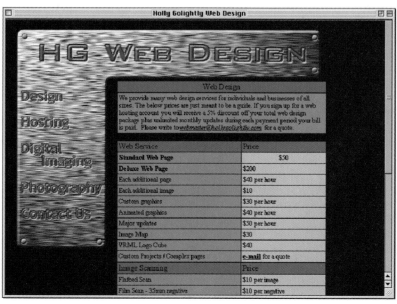

WEB.HOLLYGOLIGHTLY.COM/DESIGN.CFM

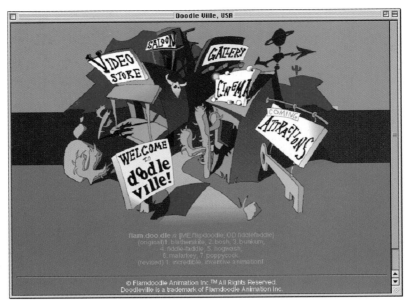

WWW.FLAMDOODLE.COM/DOODLEVILLE.HTML JEFF LAFLAMME, MICHAEL WEAVER
FLAMDOODLE ANIMATION INC. & XYNERGY INTERACTIVE | JLAFLAMME@USWEST.NET USA

WWW.JADEDLETTER.COM/
PAISLEY DALTON

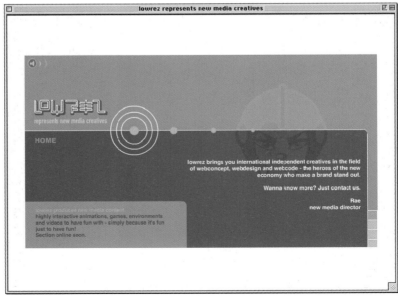

WWW.LOWREZ.NL/
LOWREZ | RAE@LOWREZ.NL NETHERLANDS

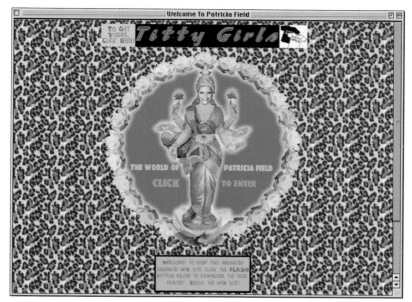

WWW.PATRICIAFIELD.COM/
DREAMSCHOOL INTERACTIVE | WWW.DREAMSCHOOL.NET   UK

WWW.MILKA.DE/COWSIM/WELCOME.PHP3
AHEAD DEUTSCHLAND | GERMANY@AHEAD.COM   GERMANY

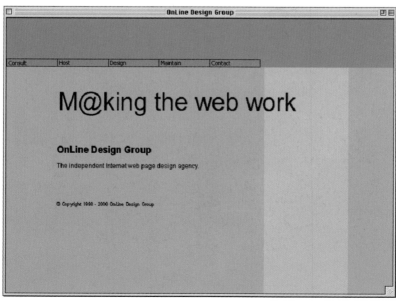

WWW.ONLINEDESIGNGROUP.COM/MAIN/

WWW.KOLLE-REBBE.DE/HTDOCS/START.HTM
INFO@KOLLE-REBBE.DE

GERMANY

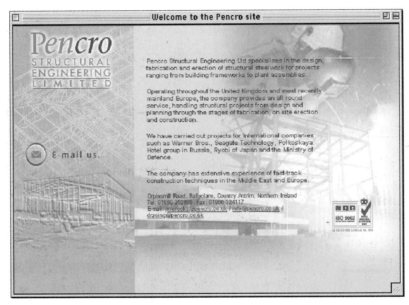

WWW.PENCRO.CO.UK/

UK

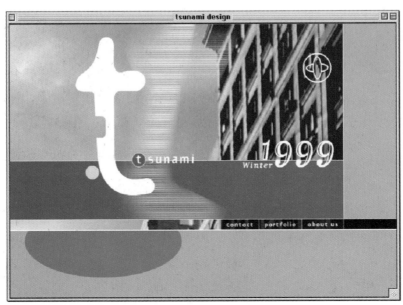

WWW.RESERVOCATION.COM/TSUNAMI/
JARRETT KERTESZ | JARRETT@RESERVOCATION.COM

USA

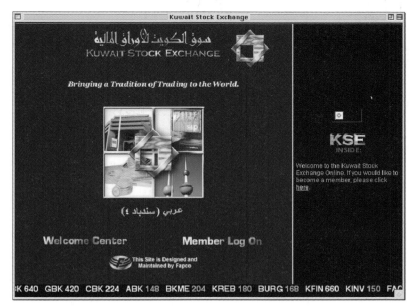

WWW.KSE.COM.KW/EN/INDEX.HTML
FAHAD AL-GHUNAIM & PARTNERSCO. | WWW.FAPCO.NET   KUWAIT

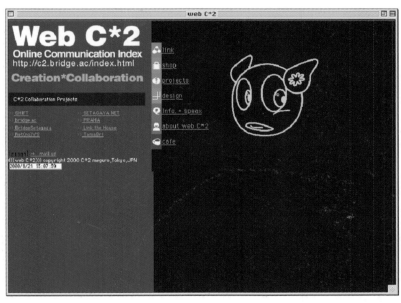

C2.BRIDGE.AC/
CHIBASHI, MIKICO, A2C | C*2 | CHIBASHI@SHIFT.JP.ORG   JAPAN

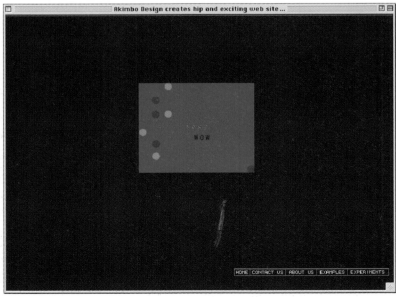

WWW.AKIMBODESIGN.COM/
BEN RIGBY | AKIMBO DESIGN | ARDITH@AKIMBODESIGN.COM

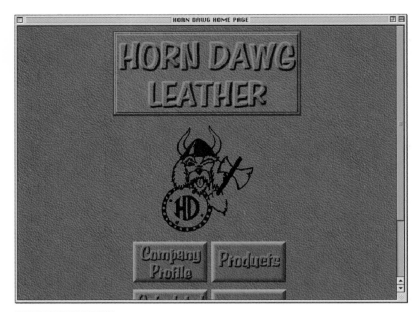

WWW.HORNDAWGLEATHER.COM/
SLOAN GOMEZ | DREAMSCHOOL@HOME.COM   USA

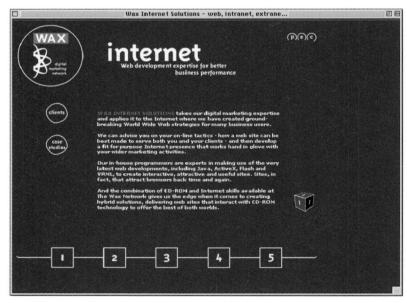

WWW.WAX-DIGITAL.COM
DANIEL BALL, LEE DELANEY | LEE DELANEY | INFO@WAX-DIGITAL.COM   UK

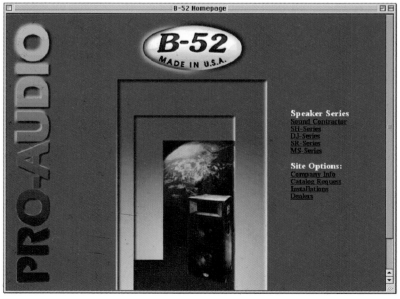

WWW.B-52PRO.COM/
JON MINNIHAN | SALES@DUNIYA.NET   USA

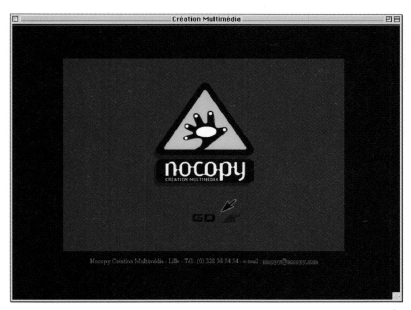

WWW.NOCOPY.COM/
NOCOPY CRÉATION MULTIMÉDIA | NOCOPY@NOCOPY.COM   FRANCE

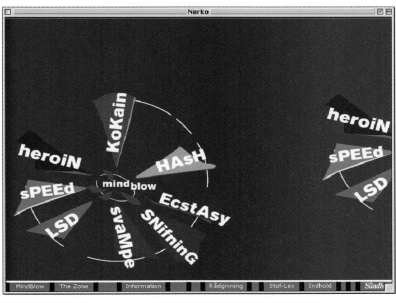

WWW.NARKOTIKAINFO.DK/   SØREN STEENSEN, JAKOB THORBEK, EBBE TINGBJERG
NETBUREAUET ARANEUM A/S | WWW.NA.DK   DENMARK

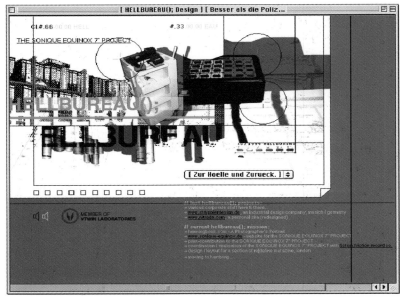

WWW.HELLBUREAU.DE/
CHRISTOPHE STOLL | NTRD@HELLBUREAU.DE   GERMANY

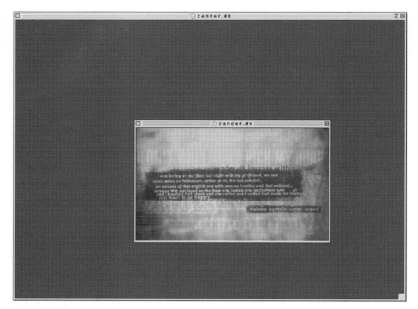

WWW.ZANDER.DK
CHRISTIAN ZANDER | Z@ZANDER.DK

WWW.KIRSANOV.COM
DMITRY KIRSANOV | WWW.KIRSANOV.COM

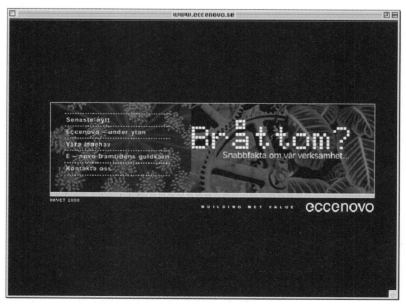

WWW.ECCENOVO.SE/FRAMESET.ASP
PÄR ALMQVIST | P@TRUEDESIGNS.COM

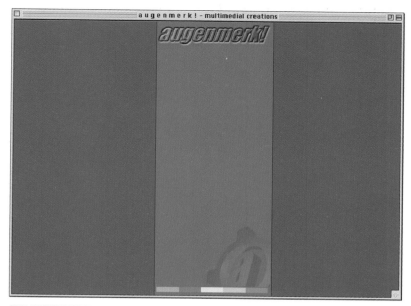

WWW.AUGENMERK.DE/ENGLISH/FRAMESET_ENGLISH_HTML.HTML
AUGENMERK! | INFO@AUGENMERK.DE   GERMANY

WWW.MEGAZIN.COM/
JOERG WASCHAT | VS.42 | WWW.VS42.COM   GERMANY

WWW.LEAFTECH.COM
ANDREW A. KUCHERIAVY | INTECHNIC CORPORATION | ANDREW@INTECHNIC.COM   USA

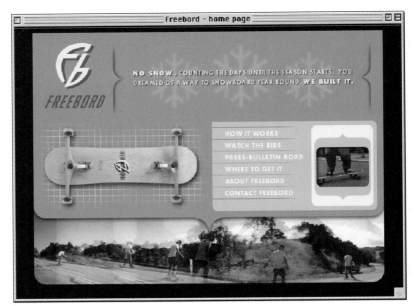

NO SNOW. COUNTING THE DAYS UNTIL THE SEASON STARTS. YOU DREAMED OF A WAY TO SNOWBOARD YEAR ROUND. WE BUILT IT.

FREEBORD

HOW IT WORKS
WATCH THE RIDE
PRESS-BULLETIN BORD
WHERE TO GET IT
ABOUT FREEBORD
CONTACT FREEBORD

WWW.FREEBORD.COM/
MATTHEW CARLSON, JULIE CRISTELLO, GUTHRIE DOLIN | BRAND A STUDIO | WWW.BRAND-A.COM   USA

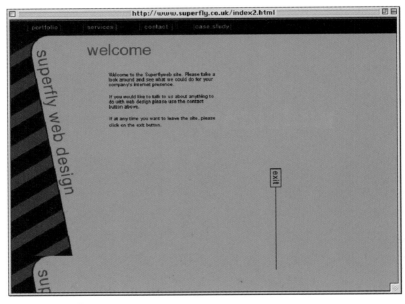

portfolio   services   contact   case study

superfly web design

welcome

Welcome to the Superflyweb site. Please take a look around and see what we could do for your company's internet presence.

If you would like to talk to us about anything to do with web design please use the contact button above.

If at any time you want to leave the site, please click on the exit button.

exit

sup

WWW.SUPERFLY.CO.UK/INDEX2.HTML
SUPERFLY LIMITED, PETER DRAY   UK

國科會數位博物館專案先導計畫 ◆ 執行單位：國立台灣大學
淡 水 河 溯 源
Digital Museum of Discovery of Tamsui River

主題展示區
Exhibitions

虛擬實境
Virtual Reality

資料搜尋區
Search

教學互動區
Play & Learn

NTUDLM.NTU.EDU.TW/WEBTITLE/PUBLISH/DEFAULT.HTM
INFO@NTUDLM.NTU.EDU.TW   TAIWAN

DS.DIAL.PIPEX.COM/TOWN/TERRACE/XAI17/
KEVIN RUSSEL

USA

FLASH.TF1.FR/ZOUGA/DEFAULT.HTM

FRANCE

WWW.AXEL-JANSEN.DE/
TORSTEN JASPER WEESE | RECOM | CHIEF@AXL-JANSEN.DE

GERMANY

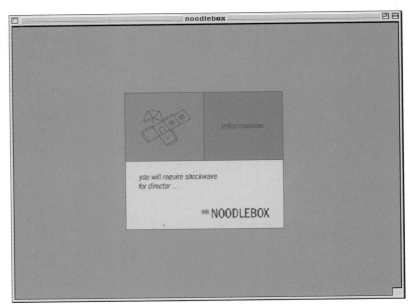

WWW.NOODLEBOX.COM
DANIEL BROWN | AMAZE LIMITED | DANNYB@AMAZE.COM UK

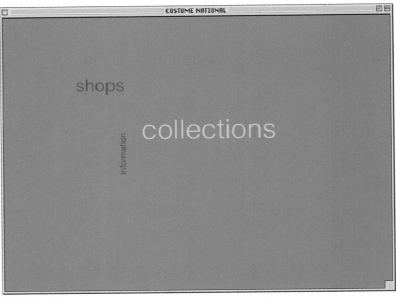

WWW.COSTUMENATIONAL.COM
PINO PIPOLI |TERMINAL | PRESS@COSTUMENATIONAL.COM ITALY

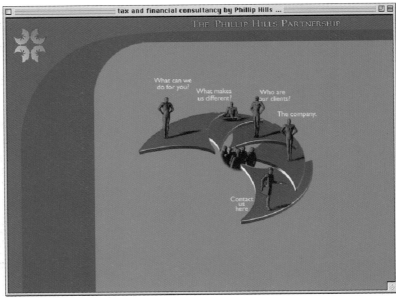

WWW.PHILLIPHILLS.COM/INDEX4.HTML
JULES CRAIG | PARADOXCAFE.COM AUSTRALIA

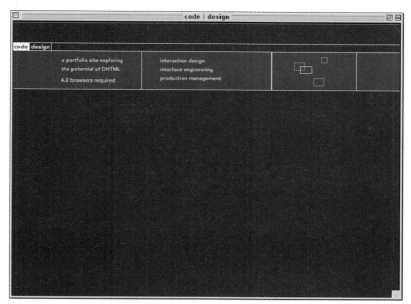

CODE-DESIGN.COM/
JOSEPH TERNES | JOSEPH@CODE-DESIGN.COM

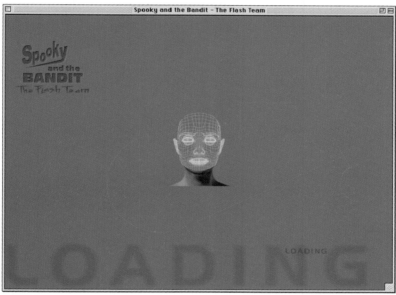

WWW.SPOOKYANDTHEBANDIT.COM

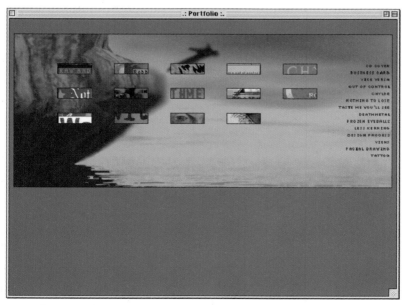

WWW.DESIGNMONTAGE.COM/PORTFOLIO/INDEX.HTML

WWW.PSYGNOSIS.COM/

UK

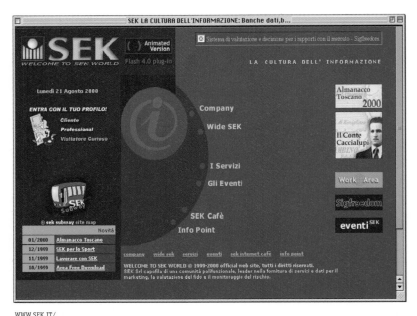

WWW.SEK.IT/
FRANCESCO SAMMARCO

ITALY

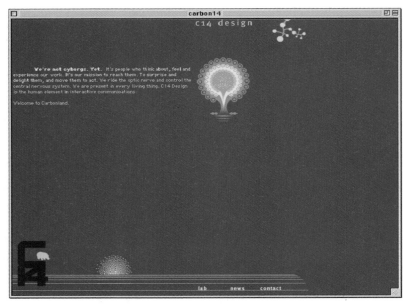

WWW.CARBON14.NET/POSTCARD.HTML
DAVE BRAVENEC | C14 DESIGN THE CREATIVE LAB OF KICK MEDIA | DBRAVENEC@CARBON14.NET   USA

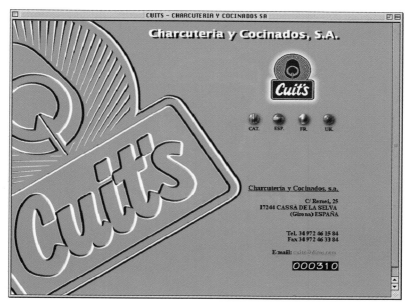

WWW.6TEMS.COM/CUITS/

SPAIN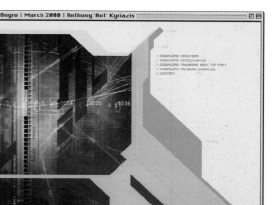

WWW.ONYRO.COM/
ANTHONY KYRIAZIS

UK

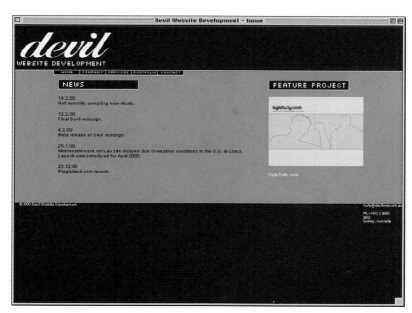

WWW.DEVILWEB.COM.AU/

AUSTRALIA

WWW.BROKENSILENCE.DE/
KLAUS SCHAEFERS | KLAUS@VOMMOND.DE   GERMANY

W3.DATANET.HU/~DRPAPA/INDEX1.HTM
KOSMAS PAPAGIANNIS

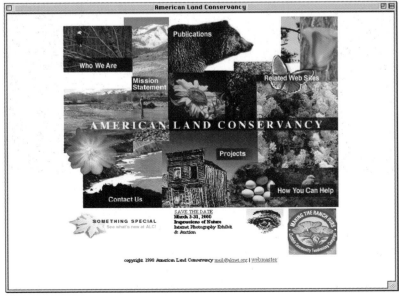

WWW.ALCNET.ORG/INDEXNORMAL.HTML

256

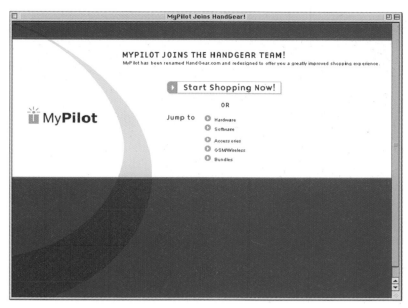

STORE.HANDGEAR.COM/MYPILOT/
NICOLE BAILON, JEROME DEL MUNDO | CRESENDA WIRELESS | WWW.CRESENDA.COM

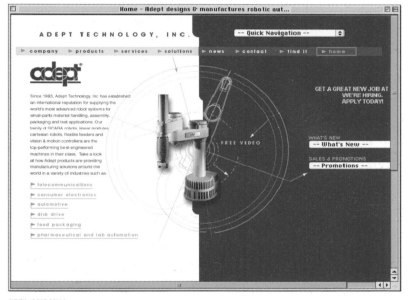

WWW.ADEPT.COM/

HEM.PASSAGEN.SE/POZEIDON/FRANCO/INDEX1.HTML
ALEXANDER PETTERSSON | ONTOYOSHIRO@RSUB.COM

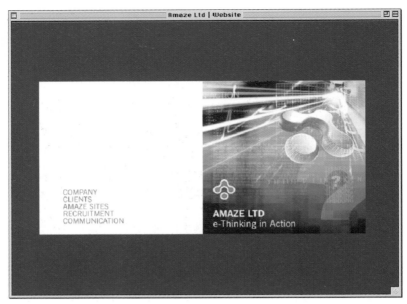

WWW.AMAZE.CO.UK/DEFAULT.HTM ADAM TODD, PAUL MUSGRAVE, MARK RAMSAY
AMAZE PRODUCTION TEAM | SITEDESIGNERS@AMAZE.COM UK

WWW.WRIGHTDESIGNS.COM/CCSC/
RANDALL WRIGHT | WRIGHT DESIGNS | INFO@WRIGHTDESIGNS.COM USA

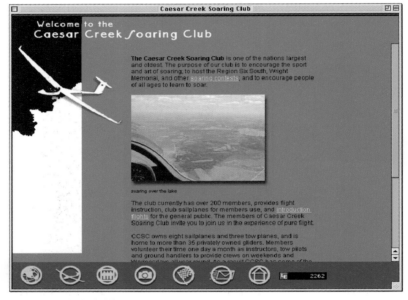

WWW.BOTSCHAFT-FRANKREICH.DE/

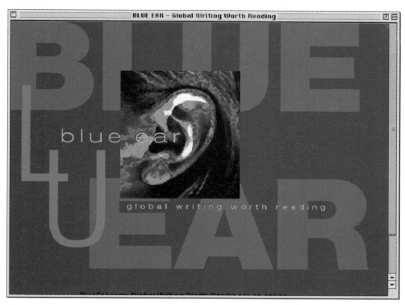

WWW.BLUEEAR.COM/
STEVE LANIER, MADELEINE MORRIS | PUBLISHER@BLUEEAR.COM

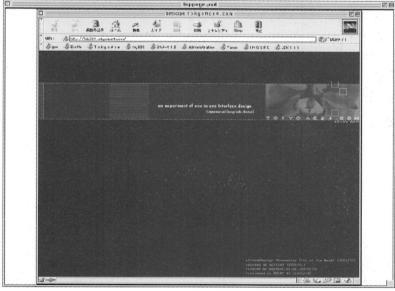

WWW.TOKYOACE4.COM/INDEX.CGI
TOHSAKI HISAYOSHI | FOURSEAS@YK.RIM.OR.JP   JAPAN

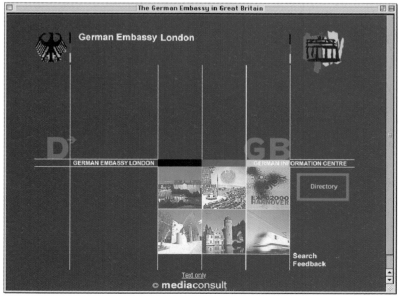

WWW.GERMAN-EMBASSY.ORG.UK/   MALCOLM MCADAM & MATTHEW TIDBURY
INTERACTIVE MEDIA DESIGN CONSULTANTS | WWW.IMDC.CO.UK>   UK

WWW.BRAINSTORMER.COM/
WILLIAM GETS | WILLIAM@BRAINSTORM.CO.ZA   SOUTH AFRICA

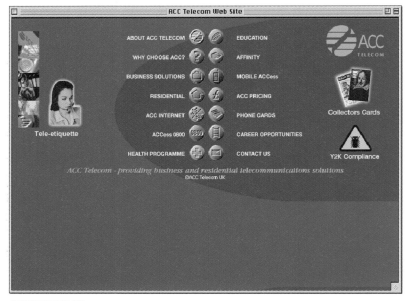

WWW.WEBADDRESS.COM
DESIGNER DESIGNERMAN | DESIGN COMPANY   UK

WWW.VOLUMEONE.COM/99WINTER/INDEXFLASH.HTML
MATT OWENS | INFO@VOLUMEONE.COM

WWW.PROJECTBOX.COM/
KRISAKORN TANTITEMIT | MODERNDOG@HOTMAIL.COM

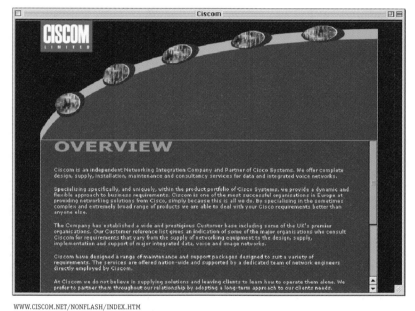

WWW.CISCOM.NET/NONFLASH/INDEX.HTM
DAVE LUIS | NEW MEDIA ONE LTD | INFO@NM1.CO.UK   UK

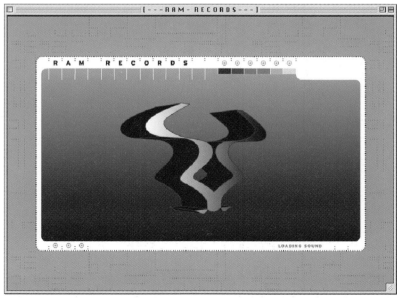

WWW.RAMRECORDS.COM/
ARRON BLEASDALE | REFORMS* | WWW.REFORMS.NET

WWW.EUROPCAR.DE/
CHANTHASENE SANANIKONE | SINNERSCHRADER AG

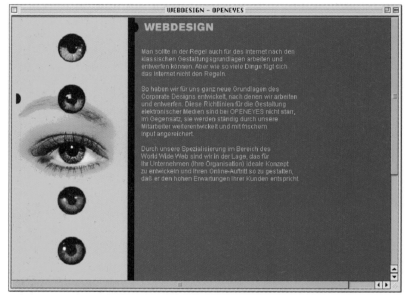

WWW.OPENEYES.COM/WEBDESIGN.HTM

GERMANY

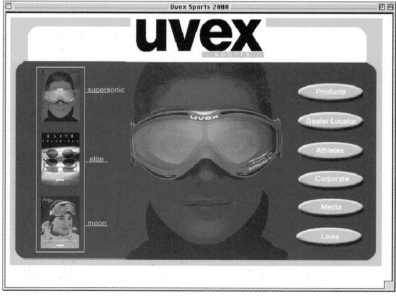

WWW.UVEXSPORTS.COM/

USA

WWW.BLOGGER.COM/

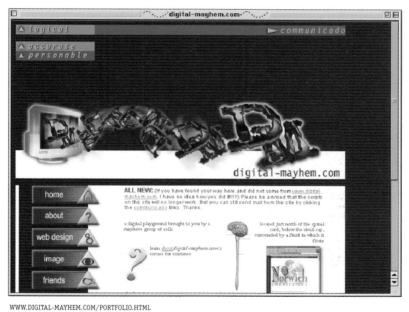

WWW.DIGITAL-MAYHEM.COM/PORTFOLIO.HTML
JAMES J. JORDAN | JAMES@DIGITAL-MAYHEM.COM   ISRAEL

WWW.FREERECORDSHOP.NL/FRSSHOP/DEFAULT.ASP
NETGATE | OFFICE@NETGATE.NL   NETHERLANDS

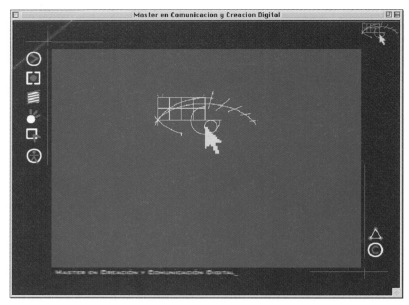

MCCD.UDC.ES/
MCCD@UDC.ES

SPAIN

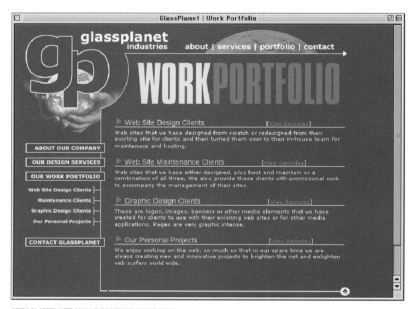

WWW.GLASSPLANET.COM/2K/PORTFOLIO/INDEX.HTML
GLASS PLANET INDUSTRIES | WWW.GLASSPLANET.COM

UK

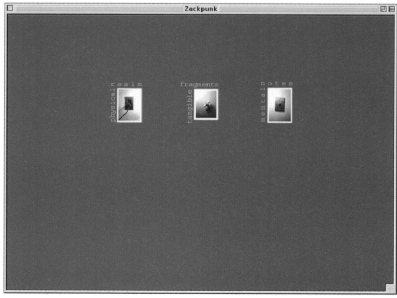

WWW.ZACKPUNK.NET/ZACKPUNK/INTRO.HTML
ZACK@ZACKPUNK.NET

WWW.PIONEERFUNDS.COM/

WWW.JEFFHOBRATH.COM/
JEFF HOBRATH | IJAD.NET, INC. | WWW.IJAD.NET   USA

WWW.COUPONNETWORK.CA/
INFO@COUPONNETWORK.CA   CANADA

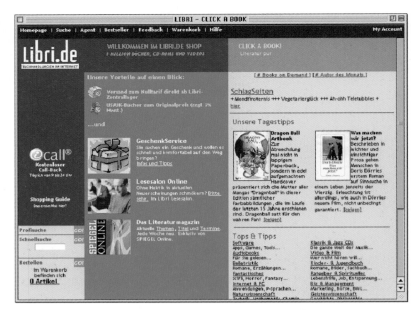

WWW.LIBRI.DE/CGI-BIN/WEBOBJECTS/LISSY?ADTRACTION=0H0H0H21   MATTHIAS SCHRADER
SINNERSCHRADER AG | WWW.SINNER-SCHRADER.DE   GERMANY

WWW.MATADOREUROPE.COM/
SALLY CREWE | X-RAY VISION | WWW.XRAYVISION.NET

WWW.BALTHASER.COM/HOME.HTML
BALTHASER STUDIOS

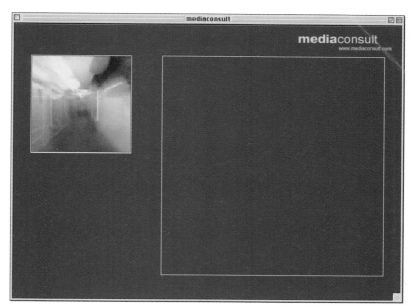

WWW.MEDIACONSULT.COM/

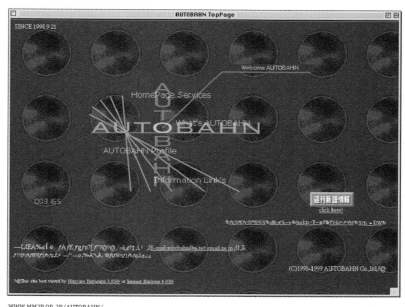

WWW.MMJP.OR.JP/AUTOBAHN/
AKIRA WADA | AUTOBAHN@A-NET.EMAIL.NE.JP   JAPAN

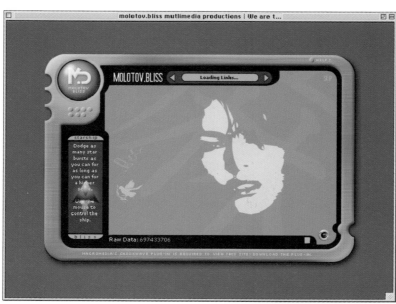

WWW.MOLOTOVBLISS.COM/
JARED BLALOCK | MOLOTOV.BLISS MULTIMEDIA | BOOMER@MOLOTOVBLISS.COM   USA

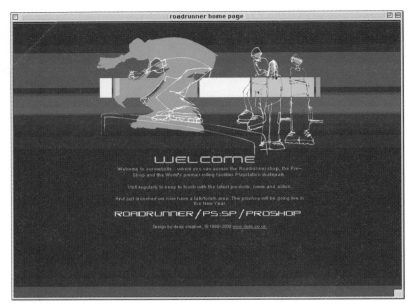

WWW.ROADRUNNER.CO.UK/
DEEP CREATIVE LTD. | WWW.DEEP.CO.UK   UK

WWW.SANDESIGN.COM.HK/
DAVID CHEUNG | SAN DESIGN (HK) LTD   HONG KONG

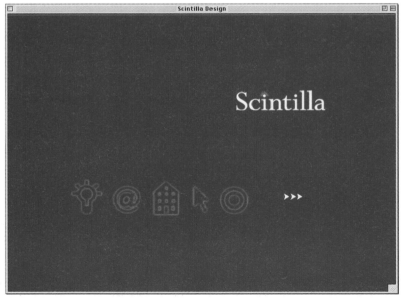

WWW.SCINTILLA.CO.UK/
10 GROUP PLC | WWW.10GROUP.CO.UK   UK

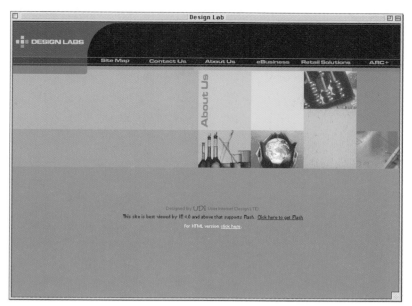

WWW.DESIGN-LABS.COM/
DESIGN-LABS | WWW.DESIGN.CO.IL

ISRAEL

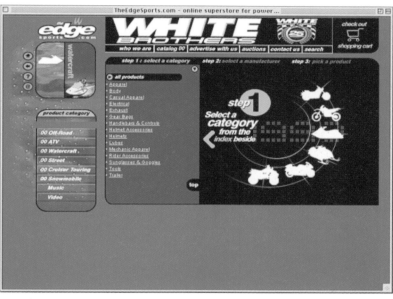

WWW.THEEDGESPORTS.COM/FRAME.ASP?SECTION=WATERCRAFT
WEBMASTER@THEEDGESPORTS.COM

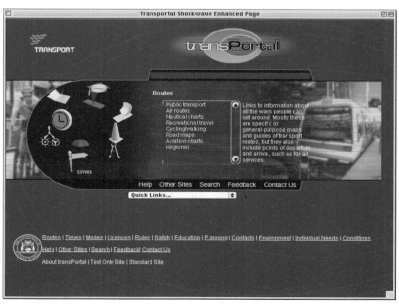

WWW.TRANSPORTAL.WA.GOV.AU/ENHANCED/

AUSTRALIA

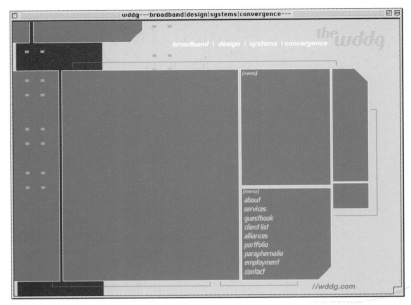

WWW.WDDG.COM/
TUAN CAO, NANDO COSTA ET AL | CONTACT@WDDG.COM   USA

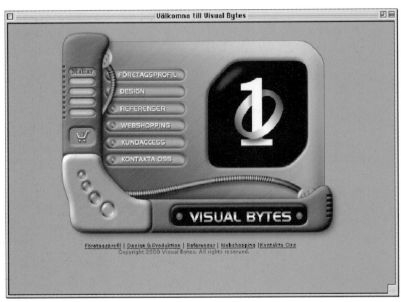

WWW.VISUALBYTES.SE/
ROBERT REHUS, LISA REHUS | VISUAL BYTES | WEBMASTER@VISUALBYTES.SE

WWW.LOUIS-POULSEN.COM/

WWW.STIMULUS.COM/V/5/HOME/INDEXV5.HTML
MARK S LOWE | IDEAS@STIMULUS.COM

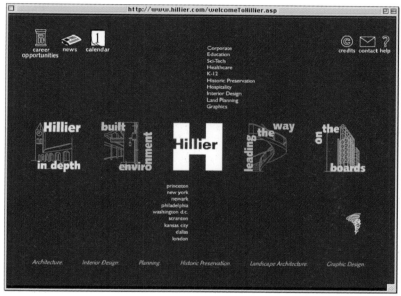

WWW.HILLIER.COM/WELCOMETOHILLIER.ASP
THE HILLIER GROUP | WWW.HILLIER.COM

WWW.LOUIS-POULSEN.COM/LIGHTING/DEFAULT.ASP

WWW.DESIGNMONTAGE.COM/

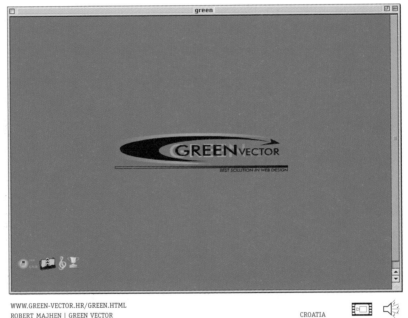

WWW.GREEN-VECTOR.HR/GREEN.HTML
ROBERT MAJHEN | GREEN VECTOR

CROATIA

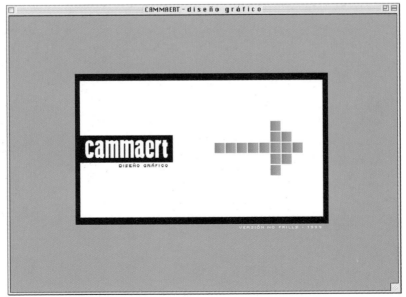

WWW.CAMMAERT.COM
JUAN CARLOS CAMMAERT

SPAIN

GLASSDOG.COM/HOMEPAGE/INDEX.HTML
LANCE ARTHUR

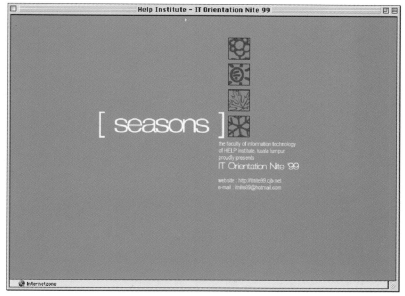

ITNITE99.CJB.NET/

MALAYSIA

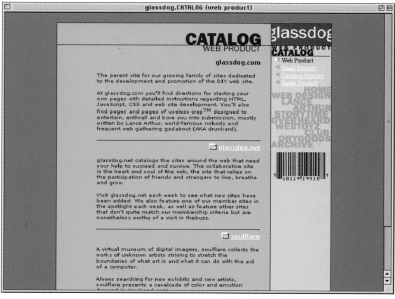

WWW.GLASSDOG.COM/CATALOG/INDEX.HTML

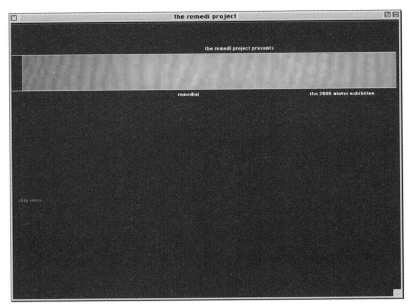

WWW.THEREMEDIPROJECT.COM/0100_SET.HTML
IORESEARCH

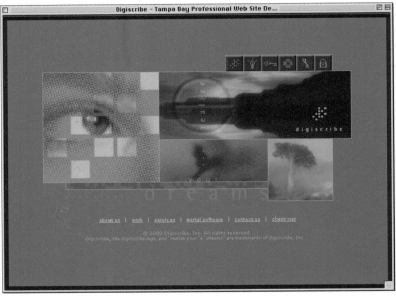

WWW.DIGISCRIBE.COM
DIGISCRIBE INC.   USA

WWW.EPB.COM/
KIOKEN INCORPORATED | WWW.KIOKEN.COM   USA

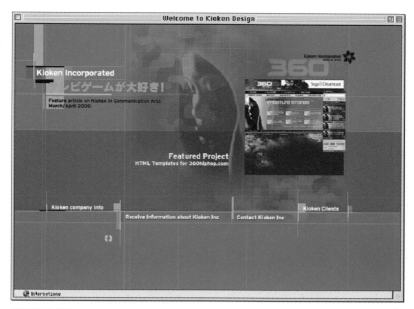

WWW.KIOKEN.COM/
KIOKEN INCORPORATED | WWW.KIOKEN.COM

USA

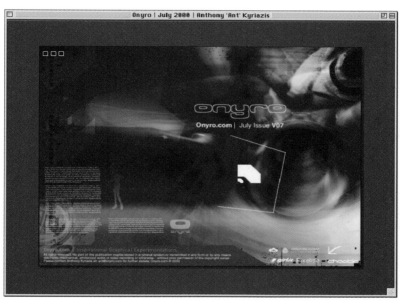

WWW.ONYRO.COM/
ANTHONY KYRIAZIS | KIOKEN UK | WWW.ONYRO.COM/

UK

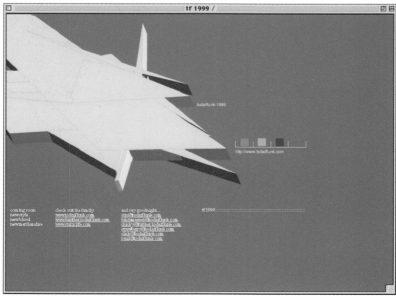

WWW.TODAIFLUNK.COM
SUN AN | 08@STATICLIFE.COM

USA

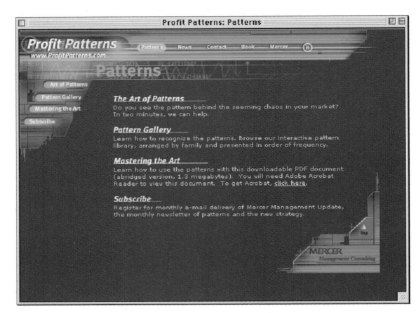

WWW.PROFITPATTERNS.COM/PATTERNS/PATTERNS.HTML

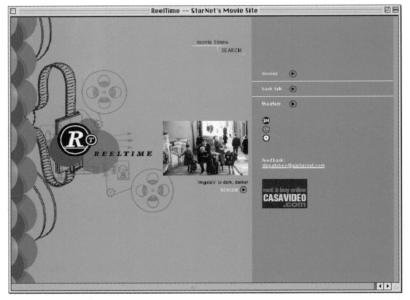

WWW.REELTIME.AZSTARNET.COM/
SEAN FITZPATRICK,WARD ANDREWS | STARNET   USA

WWW.S.DK/WEBDESIGN/

DENMARK

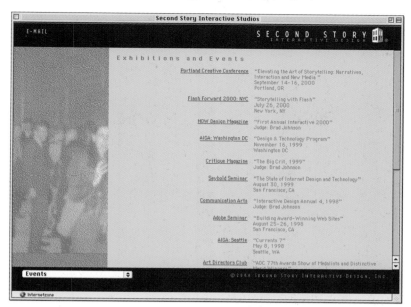

WWW.SECONDSTORY.COM/
SECOND STORY | INFO@SECONDSTORY.COM   USA

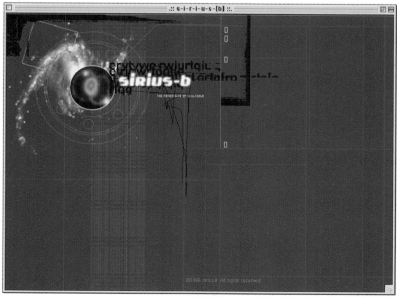

WWW.SICKOFITALL.COM/
JON RAMOS   USA

WWW.SIRIUSB.COM/
JIONG LI, DIGITARIA | INFO@DIGITARIA.COM   USA

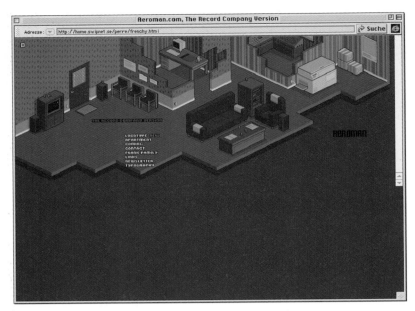

WWW.AEROMAN.COM
PERRE HOLMQVIST | P@AEROMAN.COM

WWW.MEGACAR.COM
NRG LTD. | WWW.NRG.BE   BELGIUM

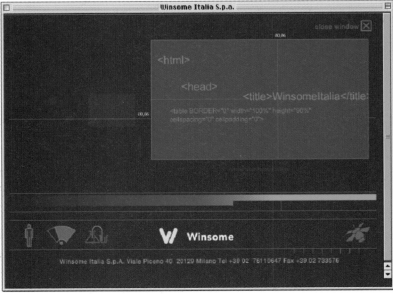

WWW.WINSOME.IT/FLASH.HTML
WINSOME ITALIA S.P.A. | WWW.WINSOME.IT   ITALY

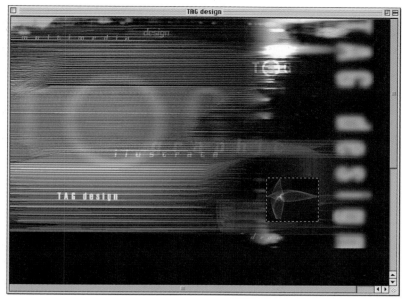

TELELINE.TERRA.ES/PERSONAL/E.PINTO/
ENRIQUE PINTO DE LA TORRE | TAG DESIGN | KONEC@OLE.COM   SPAIN

WWW.DENBYPOTTERY.CO.UK/RANGES.HTML
BROADBAND COMMUNICATIONS | INFO@BROADBAND.CO.UK   UK

WWW.IDEO.COM/IDEO.HTM

USA

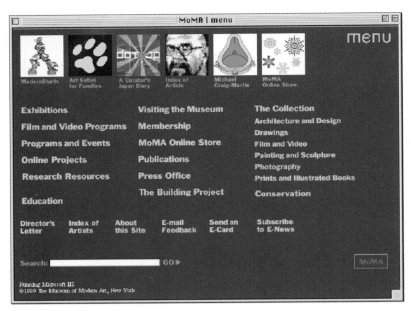

WWW.MOMA.ORG/DOCS/MENU/INDEX.HTM
ASTRIDA VALIGORSKY | DEPARTMENT OF NEW MEDIA THE MUSEUM OF MODERN ART   USA

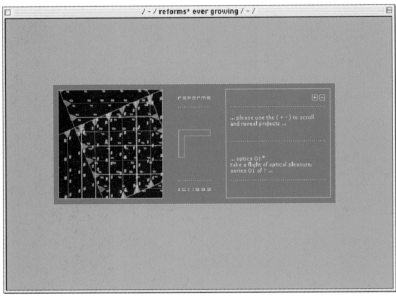

WWW.REFORMS.NET
ARRON BLEASDALE | ARRON@REFORMS.NET

WWW.DOBI.NU/DAN/DAN.HTM
DAN@DOBI.NU

WWW.DREAMTEAM.CO.UK/FRAMESET1.HTML
DREAMTEAM DESIGN LTD | INFO@DREAMTEAM.CO.UK   UK

WWW.DUNLOP.FR/

FRANCE

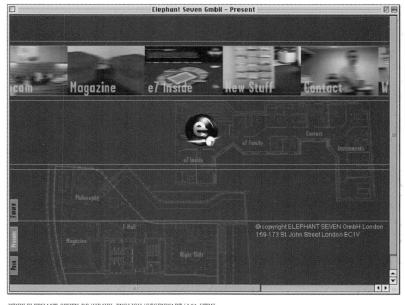

WWW.ELEPHANT-SEVEN.DE/HEAVY_ENGLISH/GEGENWART/A01.HTML
ELEPHANT SEVEN GMBH | WWW.E-7.COM   GERMANY

WWW.CONFUSED.CO.UK/
SALLY COE | FOLD7 | WWW.FOLD7.COM   UK

WWW.AIRPORT.DE/ENGLISH/INDEX/INDEX_F.HTM
VICE VERSA | WWW.VICEVERSA.COM   GERMANY

WWW.AIRPORT.DE/INDEX2.HTM
VICE VERSA | WWW.VICEVERSA.COM   GERMANY

WWW.BLUEMARLINCORP.COM/HOME.HTML
OLIVIER LAUDE AND TEAM | INFO@BLUEMARLINCORP.COM

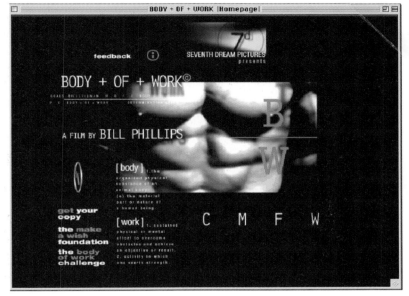

WWW.BODYOFWORK.COM/JSHOME.HTM

USA

WEBNZ.COM/IAPNZ/JOYNT/PORTFOLIO.HTM
BRIAN JOYNT | JOYNT@IHUG.CO.NZ

NEW ZEALAND

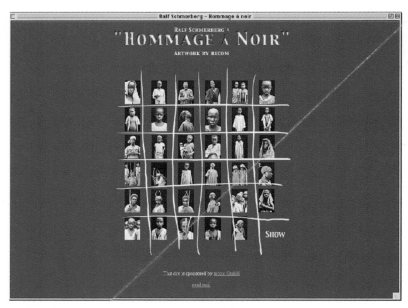

WWW.RECOM.DE/HOMMAGE/
THORSTEN "JASPER" WEESE - ART DIRECTION | JASPER@RECOM.DE   GERMANY

WWW.NCCW.NET/
GLASS PLANET INDUSTRIES | WWW.GLASSPLANET.COM   UK

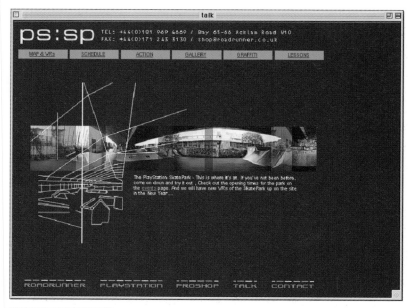

WWW.ROADRUNER.CO.UK/PSSP/
DEEP CREATIVE LTD. | WWW.DEEP.CO.UK   UK

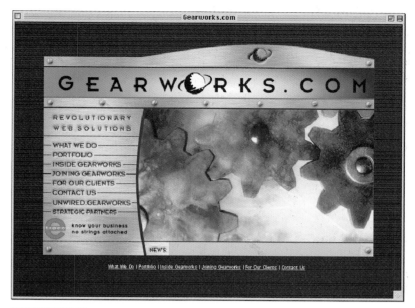

WWW.GEARWORKS.COM/
ROB DAVIS   USA

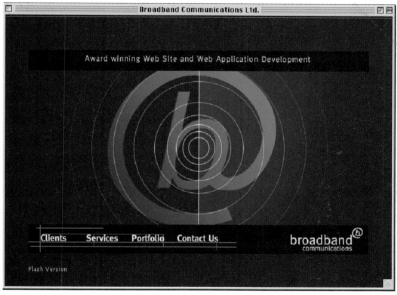

WWW.BROADBAND.CO.UK
ROBERT MITCHEL | BROADBAND COMMUNCATIONS LIMITED | INFO@BROADBAND.CO.UK   UK

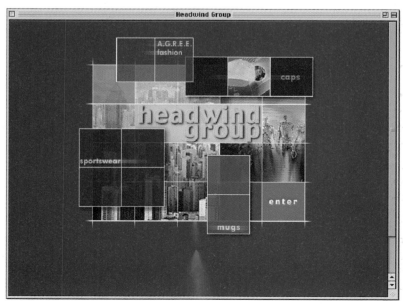

WWW.HEADWINDGROUP.COM/
PETER COHEN | OTHERWISE DESIGN,   USA

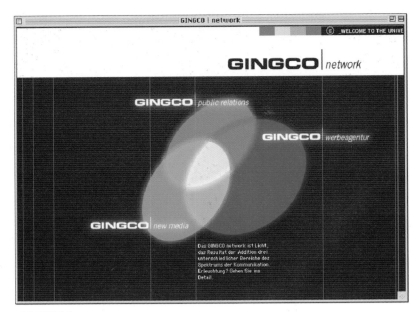

WWW.GINGCO.DE/

GERMANY

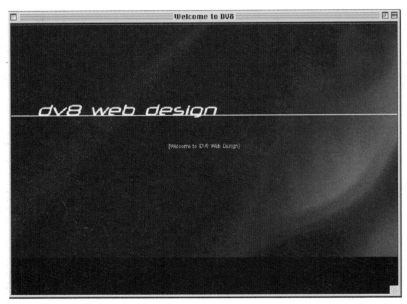

FREESPACE.VIRGIN.NET/G.HIRST/DV8.HTM

WWW.XONETIK.COM/
MARCELO PEREZ

USA

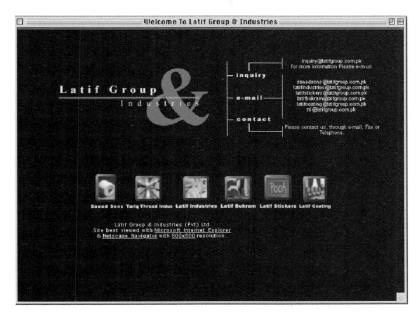

WWW.LATIFGROUP.COM.PK/INDEX1.HTM
HUMAYUN BARRY | ZIST INTERACTIVE | WWW.ZIST.COM.PK   PAKISTAN

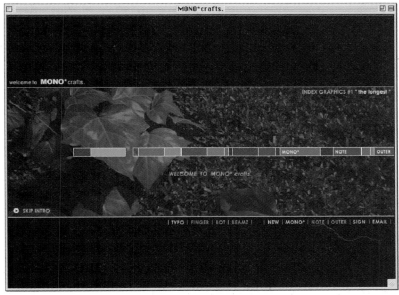

WWW.YUGOP.COM/SHOCKED/INDEX.HTML

WWW.OVEN.COM
MING THOMPSEN | WWW.MINGMEDIA.COM | INFO@OVEN.COM   USA

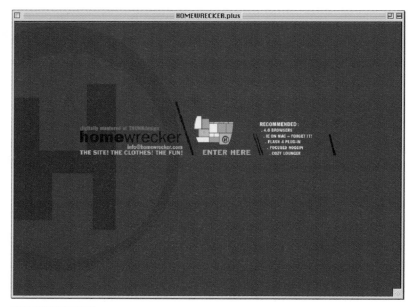

WWW.HOMEWRECKER.COM/
THUNKDESIGN | WWW.THUNKDESIGN.COM   USA

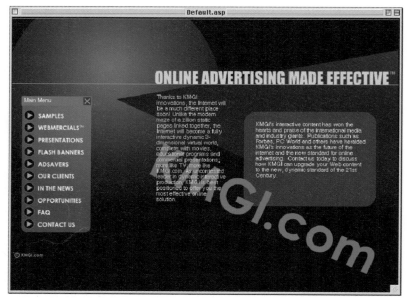

WWW.KMGI.COM/
NIKOLAI MENTCHOUKOV, KMGI.COM

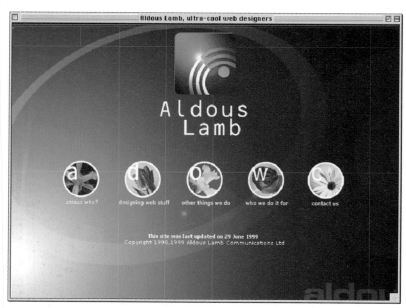

WWW.ALDOUSLAMB.COM/NONFLASH/DEFAULT.HTM
ALDOUS LAMB COMMUNICATIONS | IDEAS@ALDOUSLAMB.COM   UK

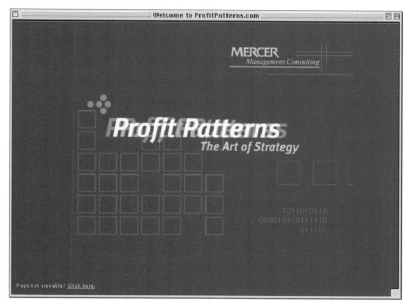

WWW.PROFITPATTERNS.COM/

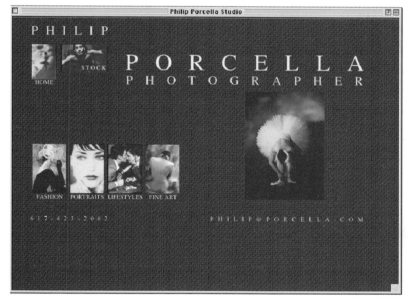

WWW.PORCELLA.COM/PORTFOLIOS/INDEX.HTML
DIMITRIS SIVYLLIS | THINKWORKS & PHILIP PORCELLA | WWW.THINKWORKS.COM   USA

WWW.MAGURA.DE/GERMAN/FRAMESET/DEFAULT.HTM
PETER BOFINGER | ACM! & 7THSENSE MEDIA GMBH | MAGURA@MAGURA.COM   GERMANY

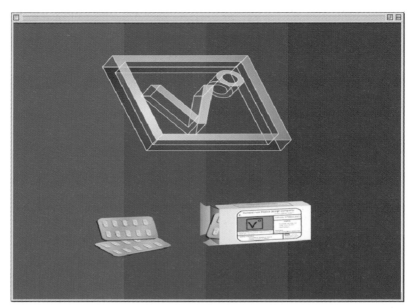

WWW.THEVOID.CO.UK
THEVOID NEW MEDIA°

UK

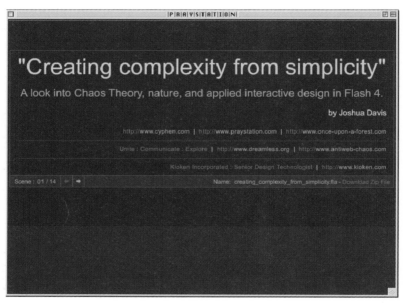

WWW.PRAYSTATION.COM/ANTIWEB/CHAOS.HTML
JOSHUA DAVIS | CHAOS@PRAYSTATION.COM

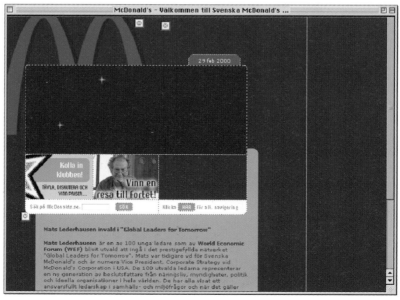

WWW.MCDONALDS.SE/
WEBMASTER@MCDONALDS.SE

SWEDEN

WWW.NAPO.DE/NAPO_NASTROVJE.HTM
JOSÉ ANTONIO GARCIA | ART-VISION | WWW.ART-VISION.DE   GERMANY

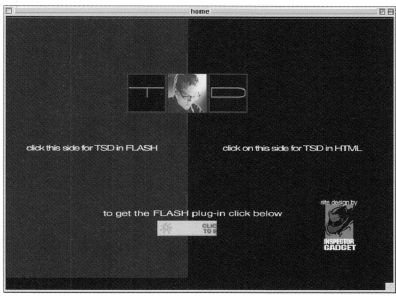

WWW.THESHEILADIVINE.COM/
SHAWN SEARS | SHAWN@THESHEILADIVINE.COM

WWW.SKIM.COM/
AREAL STUDIOS AG   SWITZERLAND

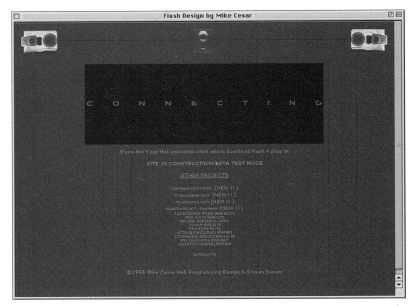

WWW.MIKECESAR.COM.AR
MIKE CESAR | ALICIA@MODELOSWEB.COM

ARGENTINA

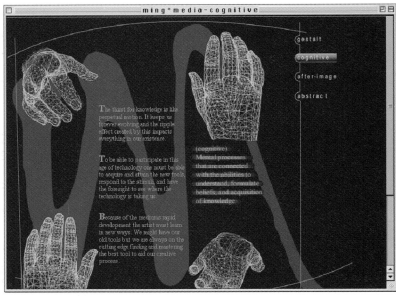

WWW.MINGMEDIA.COM/COGNITIVE.HTML
MING THOMPSEN | WEBSENSEI@MINGMEDIA.COM

USA

FIRE12.HYPERMART.NET/MAIN.HTM
WILAI JANECHAROONVONG

WWW.PELOTON.CC/MAIN.HTM
SCOTT CAMERON | DIGITAL INCITE, INC. | WWW.DIGITALINCITE.COM

USA

WWW.ODDWORLD.COM/OW_FRAMESET.HTML
ODDWORLD INHABITANTS, INC.

WWW.CRANKBUNNY.COM/
NORMA V TORAYA | INFO@CRANCBUNNY.COM

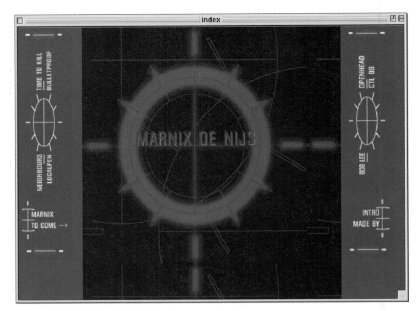

WWW.V2.NL/FREEZONE/USERS/MARNIX/MARNIX.HTML
MARNIX DE NIJS | SPLITSCREEN   NETHERLANDS

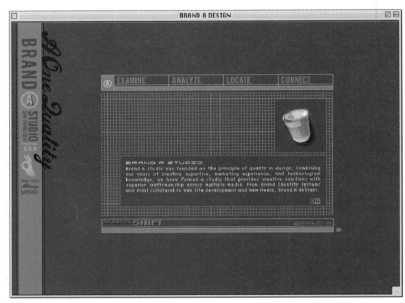

WWW.BRAND-A.COM
GUTHRIE DOLIN, MATTHEW CARLSON | BRAND A STUDIO   USA

WWW.DAVIDGARYSTUDIOS.COM
DAVID GARY | DREAMWAVE PRODUCTIONS, INC.   USA

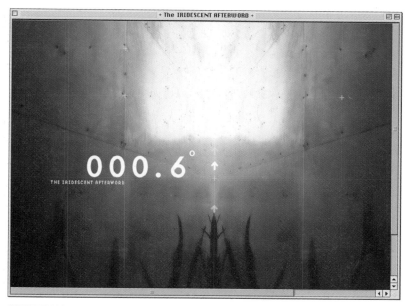

WWW.PURUSDESIGN.COM/PETAL_V2.0/FRAMES.HTML
ADRIAN LUNA | WINTER@PURUSDESIGN.COM   USA

WWW.PLASTICBAG.DE/LOGINFEBRUARY/INDEX.HTML
PHILIPP KOERBER | MEDIADESIGNTASKFORCE | POLYPROPYLENE@PLASTICBAG.DE   GERMANY

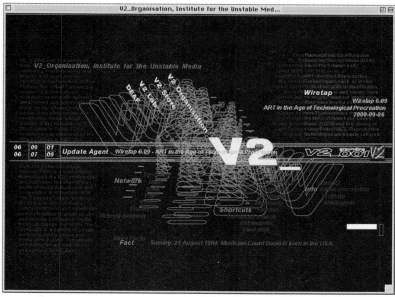

WWW.V2.NL/
V2_DIGITAL | WEB@V2.NL   NETHERLANDS

WWW.DRYMARTINI.COM
STEVEN LISKA | LISKA + ASSOCIATES | WWW.LISKA.COM   USA

WWW.XS4ALL.NL/
PETER VAN ALLER | ESTETIK@XS4ALL.NL   NETHERLANDS

WWW.FFCA.COM.HK/WELCOME.ASP
INFO@FFCA.COM.HK   HONG KONG

298

BURN.UCSD.EDU/

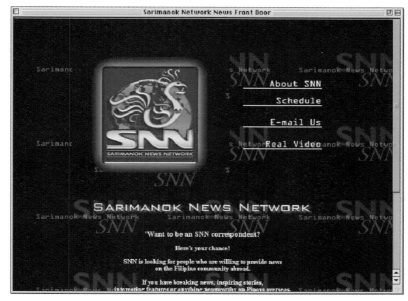

WWW.ABS-CBN.COM/SNN/

PHILIPPINES

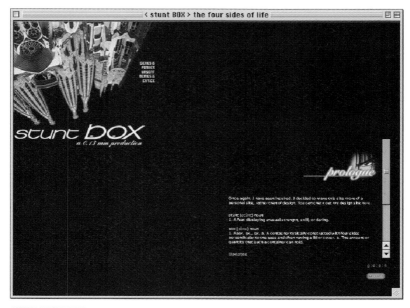

ALTEZZA.NET/STUNTBOX
MATTHEW BORDEY | STUNTBOX MEDIA LABS

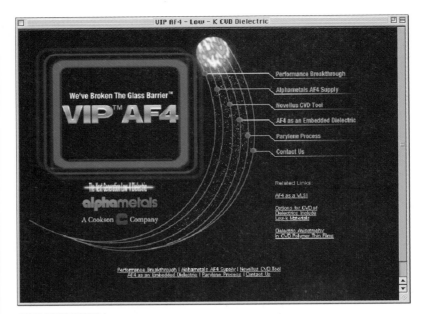

DIGITAL-MAYHEM.COM/AF4/
JAMES JORDAN

ISRAEL

HOME.HKSTAR.COM/~BENINHK/

HONG KONG

KITPROD.HYPERMART.NET/

MALAYSIA

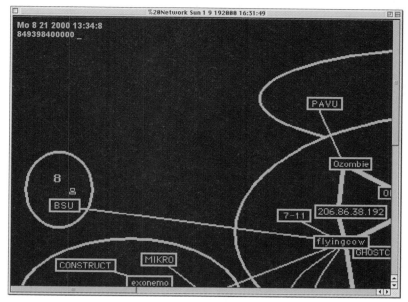

MAP.JODI.ORG/

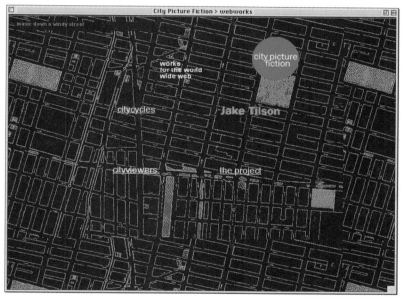

WWW.THECOOKER.COM/HERE/CITYPICT/FICTION.HTML
JAKE TILSON | ©ATLAS 1994-2000 | JAKE@THECOOKER.COM

USA

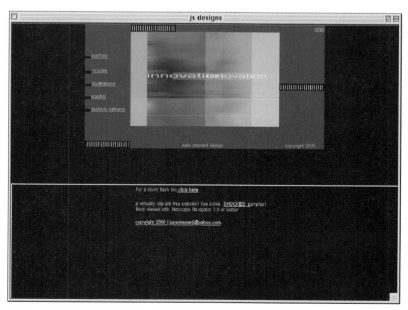

MEMBERS.AOL.COM/JUNEXX/PAGEA.HTML
BRIAN BARENIO | IRONFISH@AOL.COM

WWW.ROTKAEPPCHEN.DE/
FGK NEWMEDIATEAM | WWW.FGK.COM   GERMANY

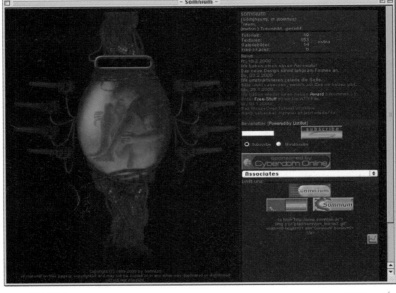

WWW.SOMNIUM.DE/
DAVID ROWALD, FABIAN BESS | S23 | WWW.S23.DE   GERMANY

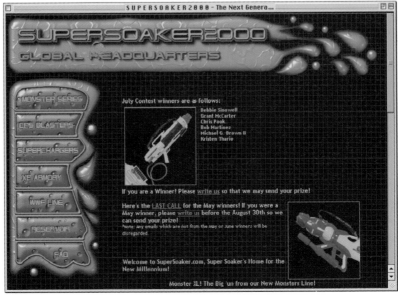

WWW.SUPERSOAKER.COM/MAIN.HTM
GERARD SULLIVAN, KIMBERLY WARZELHAN | INVERTED DESIGN | INFO@INVERTEDDESIGN.COM   USA

WWW.WEIGERTPIROUZWOLF.DE/PRE/INDEX_PLEIN.HTML
WEIGERTPIROUZWOLF & N.A.S.A.2.0 GMBH | WWW.NASA20.DE

GERMANY

WWW.TRADEGUN.DE/
JOERG WASCHAT | VS.42 | WWW.VS42.COM

GERMANY

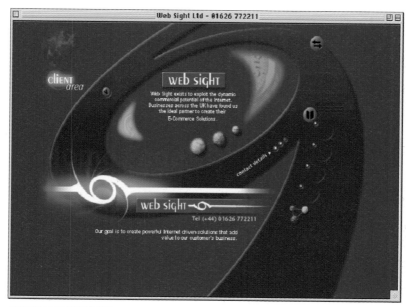

WWW.WEB-SIGHT.CO.UK/WEBSIGHT_V5/INDEX.HTML
WEB SIGHT LTD | WWW.WEB-SIGHT.CO.UK

UK

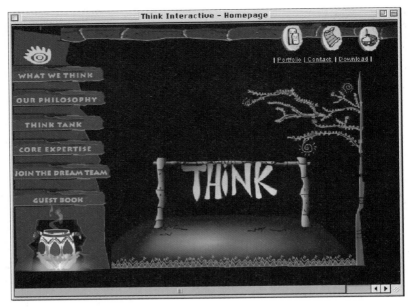

WWW.THINK-INTERACTIVE.COM/

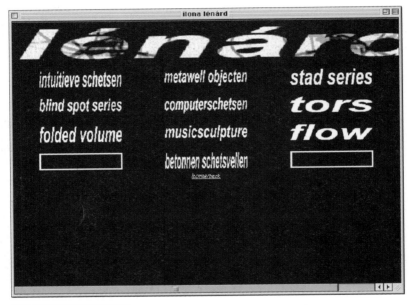

WWW.ATTILA.NL/LENARD/WORK.HTML

NETHERLANDS

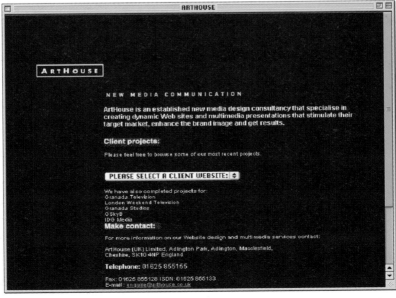

WWW.ARTHOUSE.CO.UK/

UK

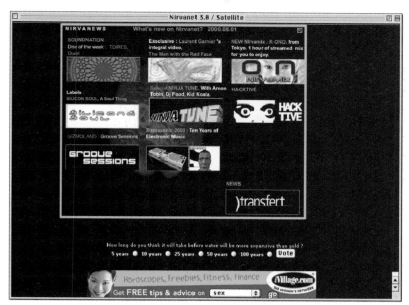

WWW.NIRVANET.COM/
PASCAL JOSEPH, FABRICE BERTRAND ET AL |REEF | JOSEPH@NIRVANET.NET   FRANCE

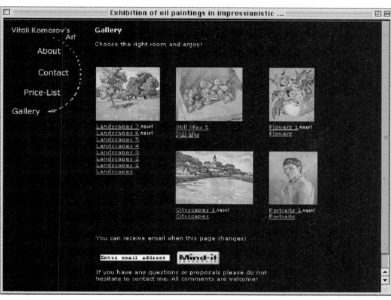

WWW.BELWEB.NET/KOMAROV/GALLERY.HTML
ALEXANDER BOREYSHA | WEBDESIGN@BELWEB.NET

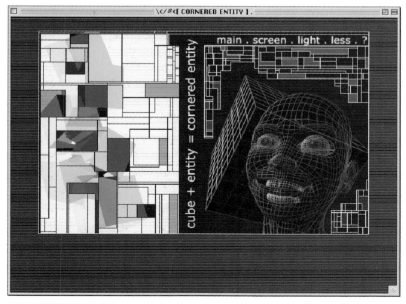

MIND.NET-SECURITY.ORG/ENTITY/
MIRKO ZORZ | LOGERROR@S1C.ORG   CROATIA

WWW.GREGOR-LUBINA.DE/MAC/MAC.HTML

GERMANY

WWW.6E.NET/
INTUITIVE.NET

UK

WWW.DDS.NL/TOER/INDEXC.HTM

NETHERLANDS

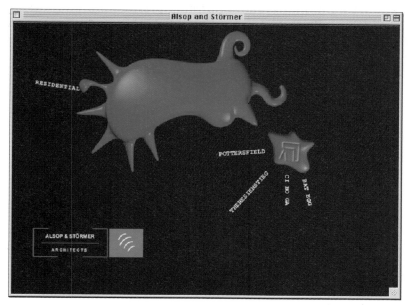

WWW.ALSOPANDSTORMER.COM/RESIDENTIAL.HTML

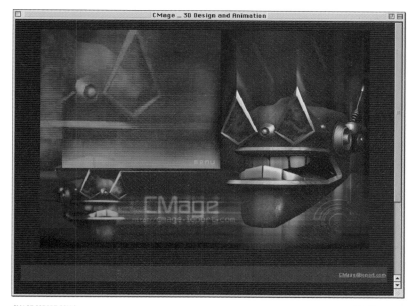

CMAGE.IOPORT.COM/
CHRIS MAGEE | CMAGE

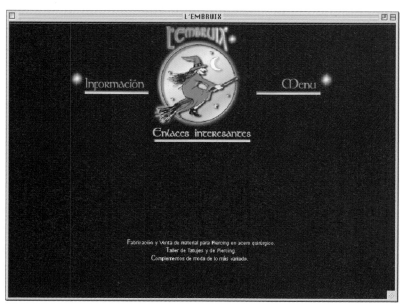

WWW.CARRIE.NET/TREMENA/
NACHO DE RAMÓN, TXEMA ARRABAL

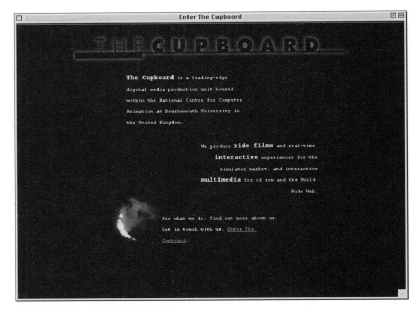

NCCA.BOURNEMOUTH.AC.UK/CUPBOARD/INTRO.HTML
PHILLIP ALLEN | THE CUPBOARD | CUPBOARD@BOURNEMOUTH.AC.UK   USA

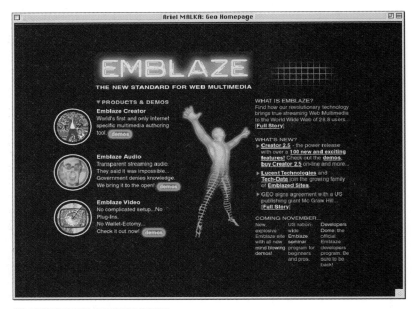

WEB4.SUPERB.NET/ARIEL/GALLERY/GEO/GEO.HTM
ARIEL MALKA | ARIEL_ML@NETVISION.NET.IL   ISRAEL

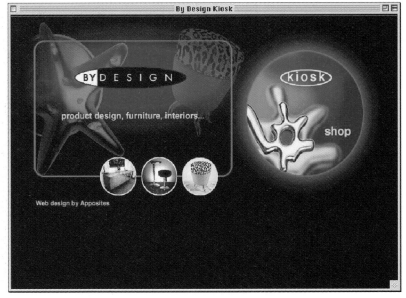

WWW.BYDESIGNKIOSK.COM/
10 GROUP PLC | WWW.10GROUP.CO.UK   UK

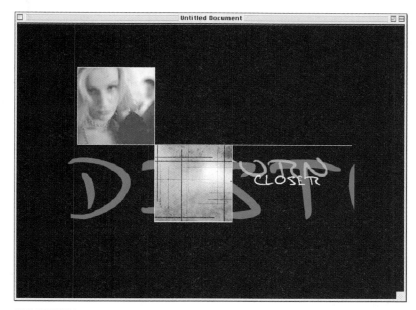

WWW.ARTEYE.COM/
JASON KIRTLEY

WWW.4AD.COM/
JOE NAVIN | WINONA DOTCOM. | WWW.WINONA-DOT.COM   UK

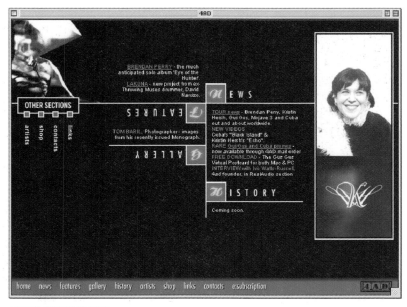

WWW.4AD.COM/FRAMESET.HTML
JOE NAVIN AT WINONA-DOT.COM | WWW.WINONA-DOT.COM   UK

WWW.KIMBLE.ORG/
NRG LTD. | WWW.NRG.BE

BELGIUM

WWW.LCI.UK.COM/
NETWORKS | WWW.NETWORKS.CO.UK

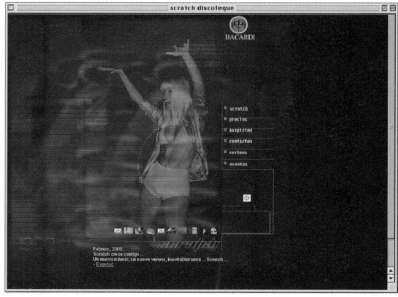

WWW.SCRATCH.CL/

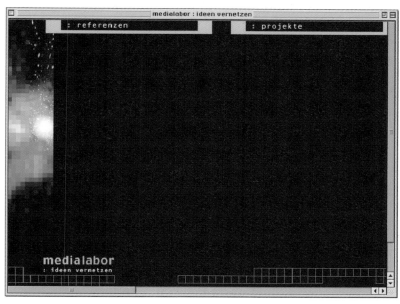

WWW.MEDIALABOR.DE/MAIN/INDEX.HTML
OLAF CZESCHNER | NEUE DIGITALE | WWW.NEUE-DIGITALE.DE   GERMANY

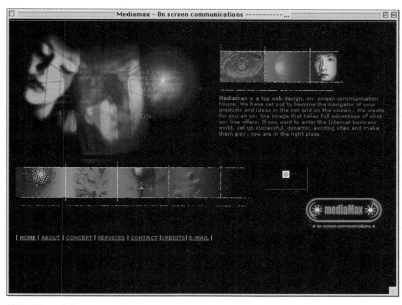

WWW.MEDIAMAX.GR/HTML_VERSION/INDEX.HTM
ALEX MOUSTRIS | INFO@MEDIAMAX.GR   GREECE

WWW.CRANKBUNNY.COM/INDEX2.HTM
NORMA V TORAYA | INFO@CRANKBUNNY.COM

WWW.TYPOGRAPHIC.COM/V02N05/INDEX2.HTML
JIMMY CHEN | TYPOGRAPHIC

WWW.GAMESTERMINAL.COM/

WWW.FREQUENCYMARKETING.COM/

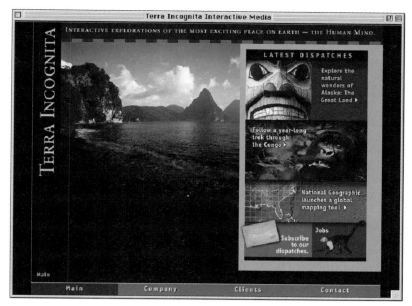

WWW.TERRAINCOGNITA.COM/
INFO@TERRAINCOGNITA.COM

USA

WWW.GOTECHMEDIA.COM/
CHARLES KWOK | GOTECH MEDIA

HONG KONG

WWW.HKS-KURIER.DE/HKS/INDEX.HTML
ADRIAN LEONARDI | WWW.CRYO.CO.UK

GERMANY

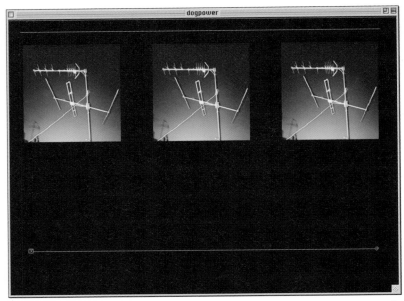

WWW.DOGPOWER.DE/MAINFRAME.HTML
FLORIAN THALHOFER | TH@LHOFER.COM

GERMANY

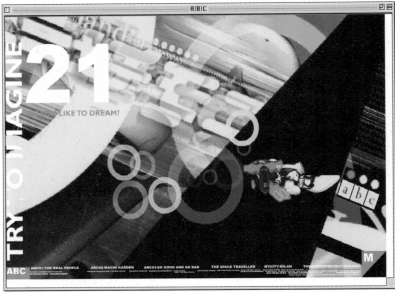

WWW.QUAM.IT/ABC/2000/LIMITED
NICOLA STUMPO | NIKO@QUAM.IT

ITALY

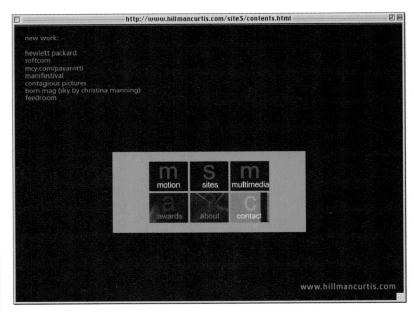

WWW.HILLMANCURTIS.COM/SITE3/CONTENTS.HTML
HILLMAN CURTIS

USA

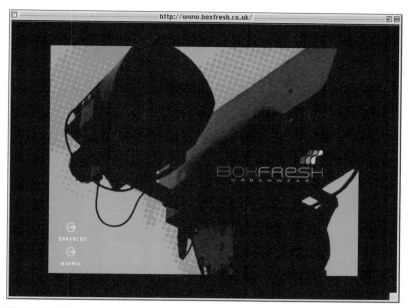

WWW.BOXFRESH.CO.UK/
ANDREW WILBOURNE, CHAKAN HISLOP   UK

WWW.FOXSEARCHLIGHT.COM/MIDFINAL/HTML/INDEX.HTML

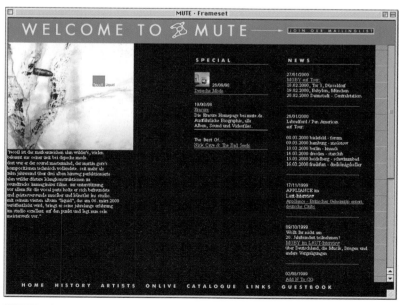

WWW.MUTE.DE/MUTE_FRAMESET.HTM
MICHAEL BOFINGER | 7THSENSE NEW MEDIA GMBH | WWW.7THSENSE.NET   GERMANY

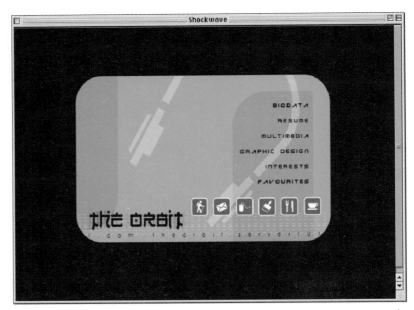

WEB.SINGNET.COM.SG/~NGADRIAN/
ADRIAN NG | NGADRIAN@SINGNET.COM.SG   SINGAPORE

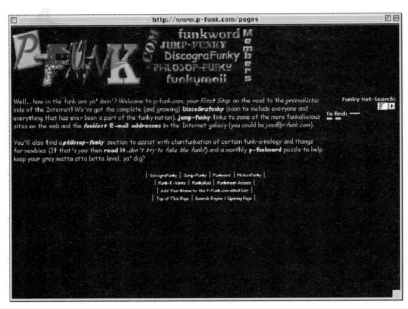

WWW.P-FUNK.COM/PAGES/
STEPHEN H. WATKINS | WATKINS AND ASSOCIATES   USA

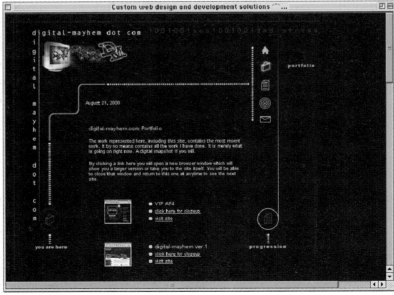

WWW.DIGITAL-MAYHEM.COM/PORTFOLIO.HTML
JAMES J. JORDAN | INFO@DIGITAL-MAYHEM.COM   ISRAEL

WWW.POSTTOOL.COM/BLAND/INDEX.HTML
DAVID KARAM | WWW.POSTTOOL.COM

WWW.HIGHFIVE.COM/CORE/INDEX.HTML

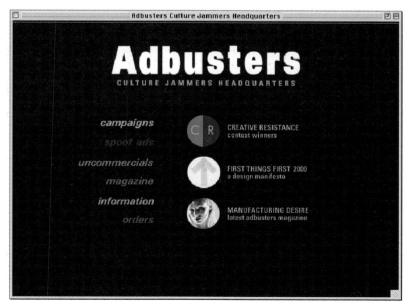

WWW.ADBUSTERS.ORG/HOME/
JEFF HARRIS | JEFF@ADBUSTERS.ORG

WWW.TRESORBERLIN.DE/AMERICA/INDEX.HTML
WILD-SITE | LABEL@TRESOR-BERLIN.DE   GERMANY

WWW.O-TEL-O.DE/WWW_TURK/INDEX.HTML
ANTWERPES & PARTNER AG   GERMANY

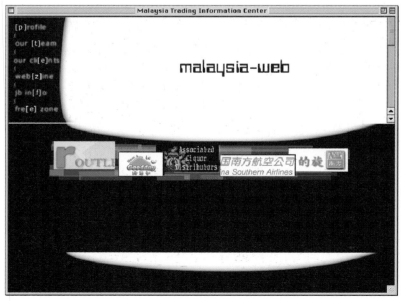

WWW.MALAYSIA-WEB.COM/
KULDDCZ@PPP.NASIONET.NET   MALAYSIA

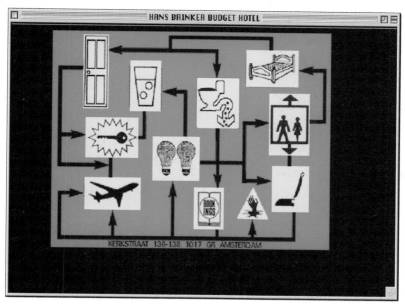

WWW.HANS-BRINKER.COM/HHOME.HTM

NETHERLANDS

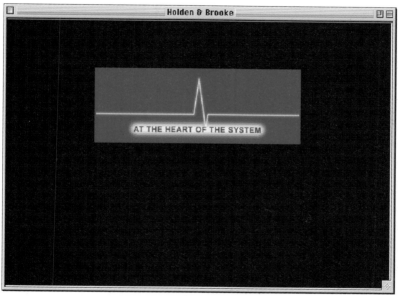

WWW.HOLDEN-BROOKE.COM/

WWW.HEADDESIGNS.COM/
JUNE STEWARD | JS DESIGN | JUNESTEWARD@YAHOO.COM

USA

WWW.PYTHONLINE.COM/NEWHOME.HTM

UK

WWW.UCHILE.CL/CULTURA/HUIDOBRO/
SISIB | UNIVERSIDAD DE CHILE.

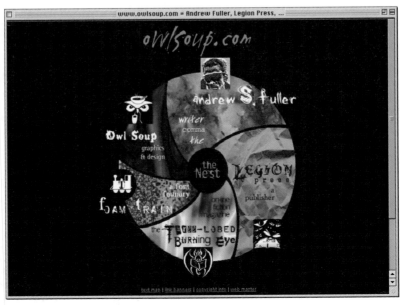

WWW.OWLSOUP.COM/
ANDREW FULLER | INFO@OWLSOUP.COM

WWW.PIMPADELIC-WONDERLAND.NEGATION.NET/70S.HTML
FANTASMA@NEGATION.NET

WWW.DDBUNCH.COM/
DINAMO DIGITAL BUNCH SRL | DDBUNCH@DDBUNCH.COM

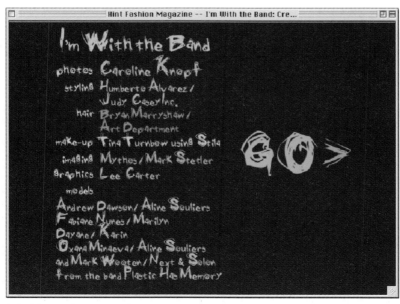

WWW.HINTMAG.COM/IMWITHTHEBAND/CREDITS.HTM
HINT FASHION MAGAZINE | HINT@HINTMAG.COM

WWW.ILLIG.COM/

WWW.HMCO.SE/BRAND/INDEX.HTM
LARS HOLMGREN | INFO@HMCO.SE   SWEDEN

WWW.RAINCHILDREN.COM/
MARTY SHAUGHNESSY

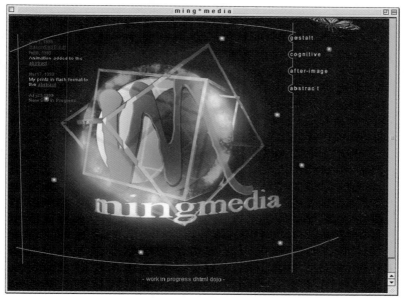

WWW.MINGMEDIA.COM/INDEXHIFI.HTML
MING THOMPSEN | WEBSENSEI@MINGMEDIA.COM   USA

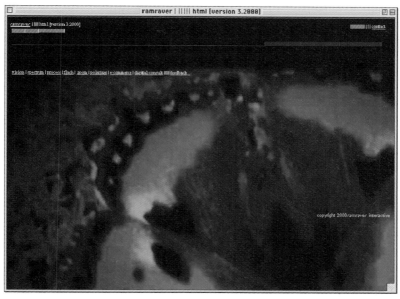

WWW.RAMRAVER.COM/
RAMRAVER   GERMANY

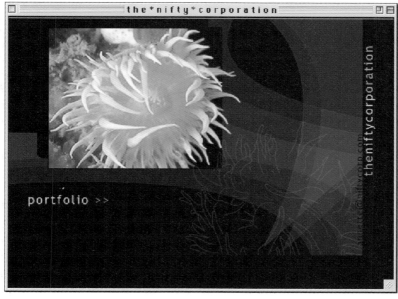

WWW.NIFTYCORP.COM

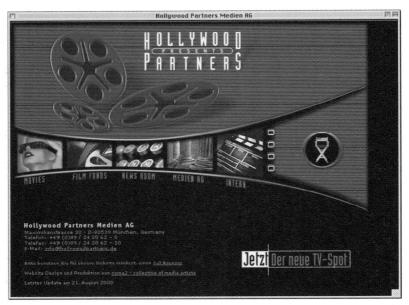

WWW.HOLLYWOODPARTNERS.DE
COLLIN CROOME | COMA 2 | COLLIN@COMA2.COM

GERMANY

WWW.PLANET.DK/
THE PLANET | BEAM@PLANET.DK

DENMARK

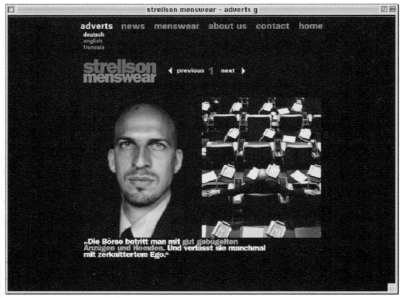

WWW.STRELLSON.CH/ADVERTS/ADVERTS.ASP

SWITZERLAND

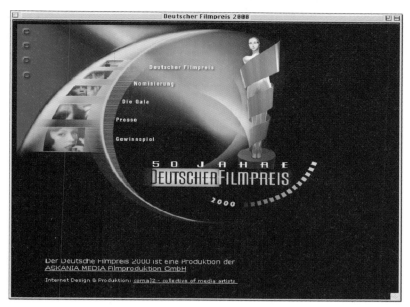

WWW.DEUTSCHERFILMPREIS.DE
COLLIN CROOME | COMA2 | COLLIN@COMA2.COM

GERMANY

WWW.SOULFLARE.COM/

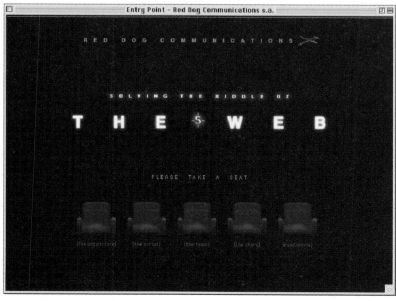

WWW.RED-DOG.COM/INDEX1.HTM
MARC VERSCHAEREN | REDDOG@RED-DOG.COM

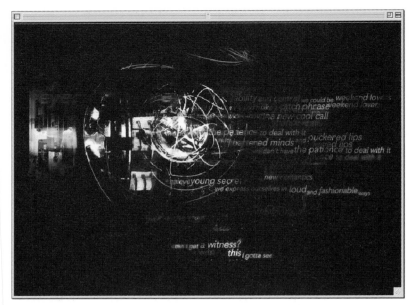

WWW.EYEDROPPER.ORG/
MAGNUS HÖGGREN | MAGNUS@KOBRA.NET   GERMANY

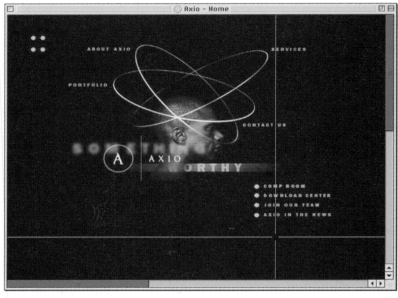

WWW.AXIODESIGN.COM/HOMEPAGE.HTM
AXIO, INC.

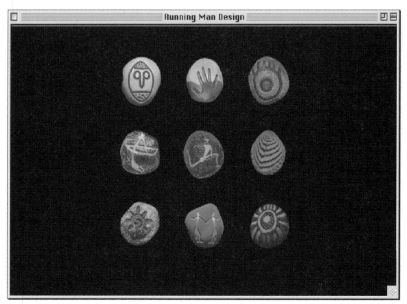

WWW.RUNNINGMAN.CO.UK/HOME2.HTM
SHAUN APPLEBY | RUNNING MAN GROUP | ENQUIRIES@RUNNINGMAN.CO.UK   UK

WWW.COMA2.COM/
COLLIN CROOME | COMA2 | COLLIN@COMA2.COM

GERMANY

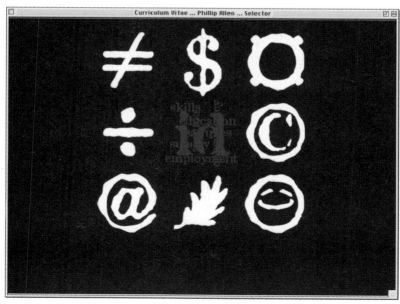

WWW.CYBERNETIC.COM.HK/CMAIN.HTM
DOMINIC FUNG | CYBERNETIC INFORMATION TECHNOLOGY

HONG KONG

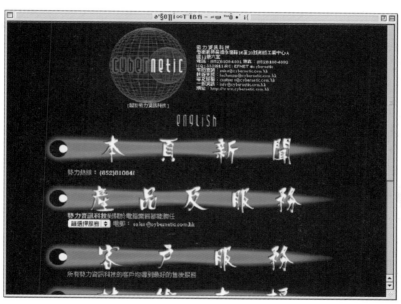

NCCA.BOURNEMOUTH.AC.UK/MAIN/STAFF/PHILL/VITAE/CARTE.HTML
PHILLIP ALLEN | CUPBOARD@BOURNEMOUTH.AC.UK

USA

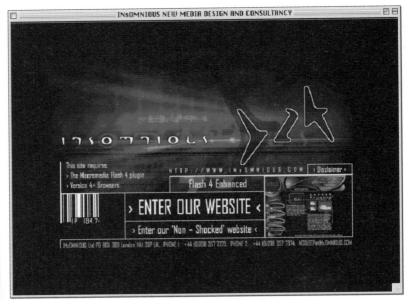

WWW.INSOMNIOUS.COM/Y2K/INDEXIE.HTM
WWW.INSOMNIOUS.COM | NOSLEEP@INSOMNIOUS.COM

UK

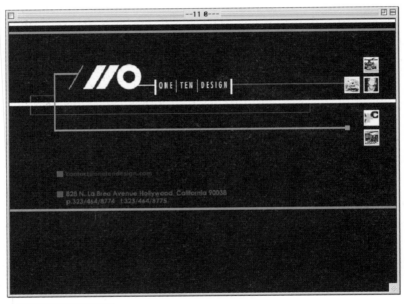

WWW.ONETENDESIGN.COM/BLACK/
GEORGE SHAW | ONE TEN DESIGN | CONTACT@ONETENDESIGN.COM

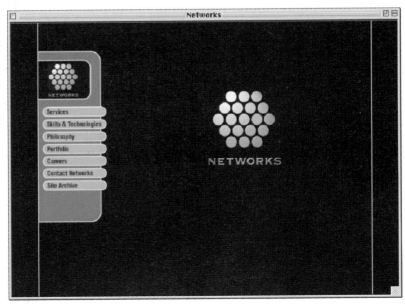

WWW.NETWORKS.CO.UK/
JERRY WERRETT, ED RICHARDSON, LISA KENNEDY | NETWORKS

UK

WWW.EFREDAGUILAR.COM/PLASTIC ALEXANDER DOLININ, CHARLES WOLFE
SUN IMAGING | INFO@SUNIMAGING.COM USA

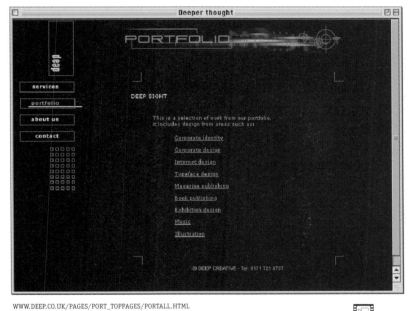

WWW.DEEP.CO.UK/PAGES/PORT_TOPPAGES/PORTALL.HTML
DEEP CREATIVE LTD. | WWW.DEEP.CO.UK UK

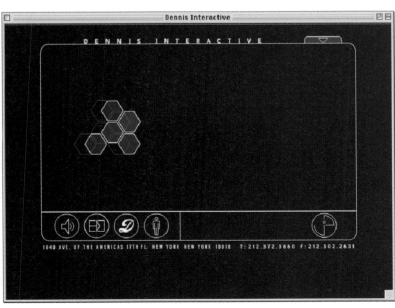

WWW.DENNISINTER.COM/DI/DISITE.HTML
INFO@DENNISINTER.COM

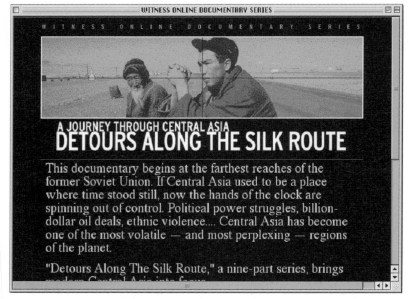

WWW.WORLDMEDIA.FR/WITNESS/

FRANCE

WWW.TIMEOUT.COM/
AREHAUS |TIME OUT GROUP

UK

WWW.FILM.COM/TOP.HTML

WWW.XSITE.LTD.UK/
WREN GILES | XSITE LTD. | INFO@XSITE.LTD.UK   UK

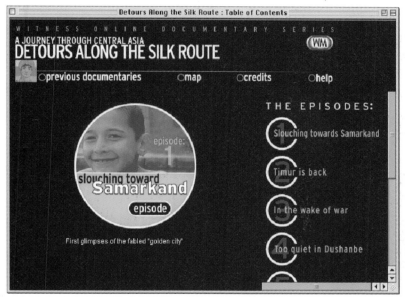

WWW.WORLDMEDIA.FR/WITNESS/III_STANS/HTML/TOC/TOC_SET.HTML
                                                              FRANCE

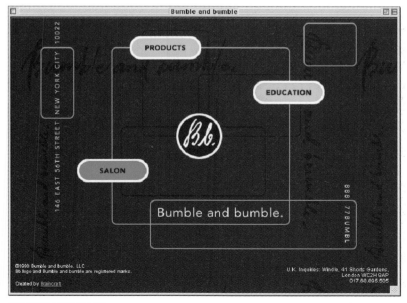

WWW.BUMBLEANDBUMBLE.COM
BRAINCRAFT | WWW.BRAINCRAFT.COM   USA

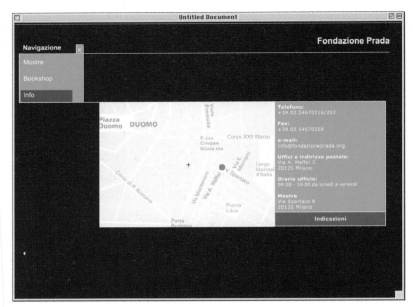

WWW.FONDAZIONEPRADA.ORG
WANDA GANATA ET AL | WINSOME ITALIA S.P.A. | WWW.WINSOME.IT

ITALY

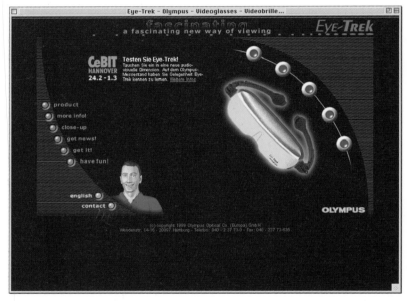

WWW.EYE-TREK.DE/
KLAUS ROSENFELD | N@WORK | EYE-TREK@OLYMPUS-EUROPA.COM

ITALY

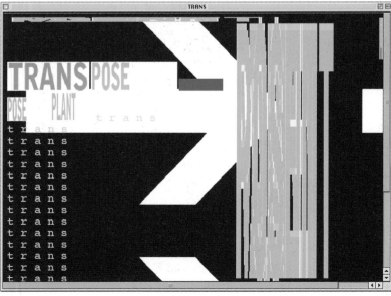

WWW.THECOOKER.COM/HERE/SOFT/TRANS/LAYERSIGN.HTML
JAKE TILSON | ©ATLAS 1994-2000 | JAKE@THECOOKER.COM

USA

WWW.THECOOKER.COM/HERE/LOOKING/LOOKING.HTML
JAKE TILSON | ©ATLAS 1994-2000 | JAKE@THECOOKER.COM

USA

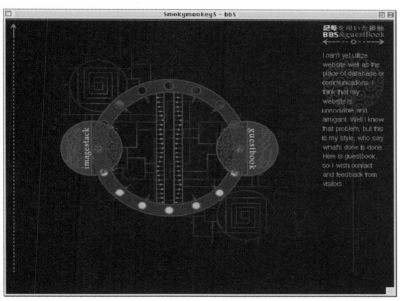

WWW.HANUMAN.CO.JP/MONKEYS/
KOIZUMI TOTA | SMOKYMONKEYS@HANUMAN.CO.JP

JAPAN

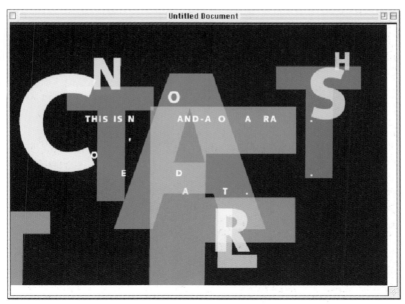

LGFACTORY.COM/SAL.HTM
THE LOOKING GLASS FACTORY

ITALY

WWW.JADE.DTI.NE.JP/~ALPHAX/TOP.HTM

JAPAN

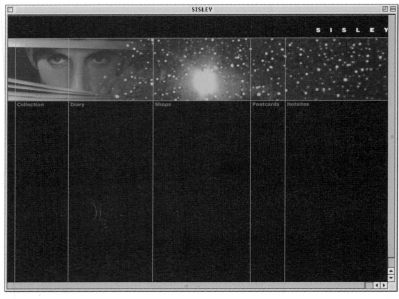

WWW.SISLEY.COM/INDEX1.HTML
WANDA GANATA, ET AL | WINSOME ITALIA S.P.A. | WWW.WINSOME.IT

ITALY

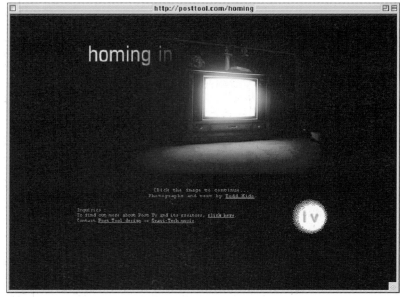

WWW.POSTTOOL.COM/HOMING
DAVID KARAM | WWW.POSTTOOL.COM

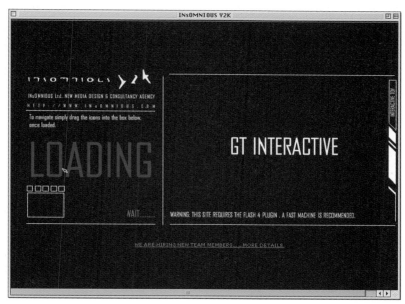

WWW.INSOMNIOUS.COM/Y2K/INSOMNIOUS.HTM
WWW.INSOMNIOUS.COM | NOSLEEP@INSOMNIOUS.COM UK

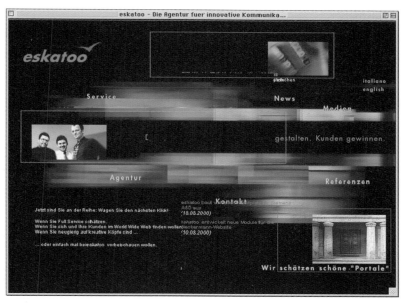

WWW.ESKATOO.DE/
GEORG STIEGLER, ESKATOO | WIESENBURG@ESKATOO.DE GERMANY

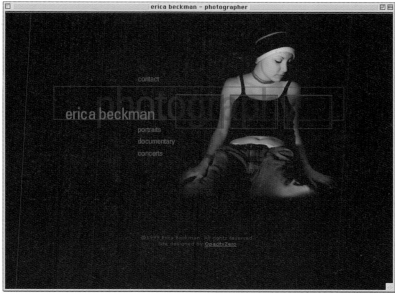

WWW.OPACITYZERO.COM/ERICA/
ERICA BECKMAN, CHRISTINE PILLSBURY | US INTERACTIVE | WWW.OPACITYZERO.COM USA

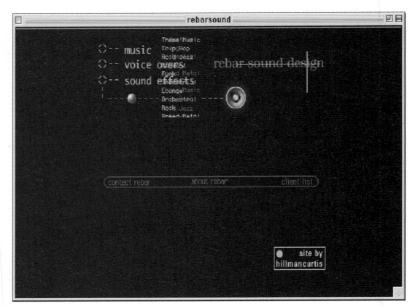

WWW.REBARSOUND.COM/HTML/MAIN.HTM

WWW.RED-DOG.COM/BIGPICT/INDEX.HTM
MARC VERSCHAEREN | REDDOG@RED-DOG.COM

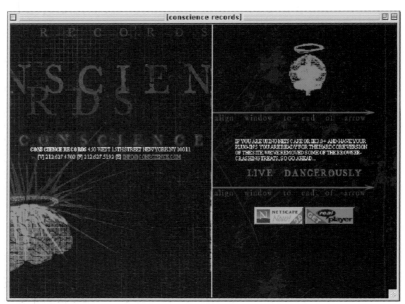

WWW.CONSCIENCE.COM/
AURIEA HARVEY | ENTROPY8 DIGITAL DESIGNWWW.ENTROPY8.COM | INFO@CONSCIENCE.COM

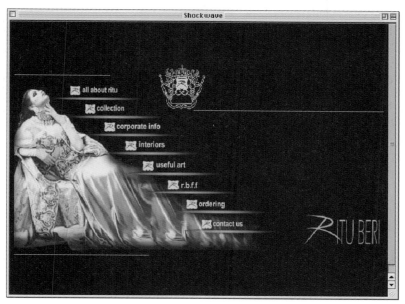

WWW.RITUBERI.COM/FLASH/HOMEPAGE.HTM

ITALY

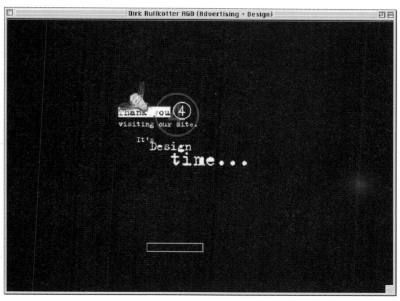

WWW.RULLKOETTER.DE
DIRK RULLKOETTER | INFO@RULLKOETTER.DE

GERMANY

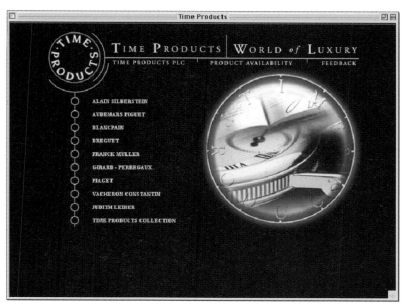

WWW.TIMEPRODUCTS.CO.UK/

UK

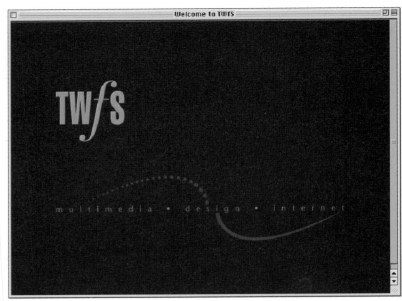

WWW.TWFS.CO.UK/
NICK MAKEY | TWFS | INFO@TWFS.CO.UK   UK

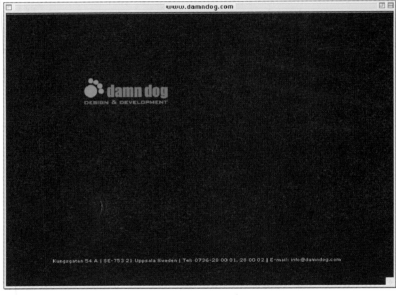

WWW.DAMNDOG.COM
DAMN DOG DESIGN & DEVELOPMENT | INFO@DAMNDOG.COM

WWW.QUESTACON.EDU.AU/INDEX.HTML
BRENTON HONEYMAN | BRENTON.HONEYMAN@QUESTACON.EDU.AU   AUSTRALIA

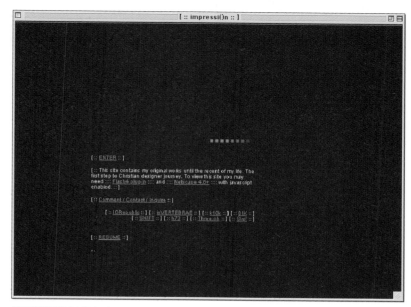

WWW.UWINNIPEG.CA/~BKWAN/
BILLY KWAN | BILLYKWAN@MAIL.COM

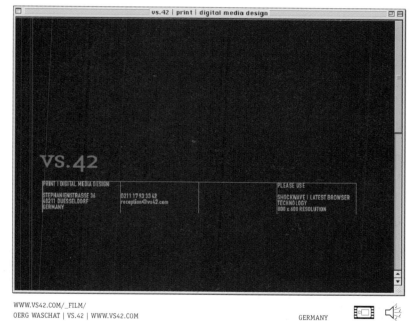

WWW.VS42.COM/_FILM/
OERG WASCHAT | VS.42 | WWW.VS42.COM

GERMANY

WWW.WEBSTORE.FR/HOME/ANIMATION.HTM
INFO@WEBSTORE.FR

FRANCE

BERRINGA.COM/INTRO/BERRINGA.HTM
JAMES LEAL-VALIAS | BERRINGA MEDIA | INFO@BERRINGA.COM   CANADA

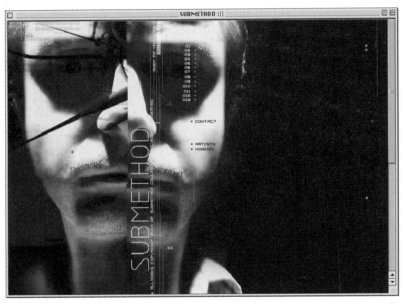

WWW.SUBMETHOD.COM
SUBMETHOD   USA

WWW.JPGAULTIER.FR/PAGES/FR/COUTURE/HIVER00/INDEX.HTML
RAPHAEL ELIG | RELIG@ECHOSYSTEM.COM   FRANCE

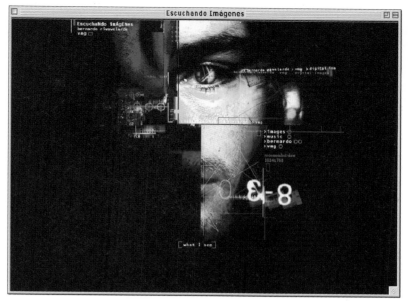

WWW.ICONMEDIALAB.ES/EI/10/10.HTML
BERNARDO RIVAVELARDE | WWW.ICONMEDIALAB.ES   SPAIN

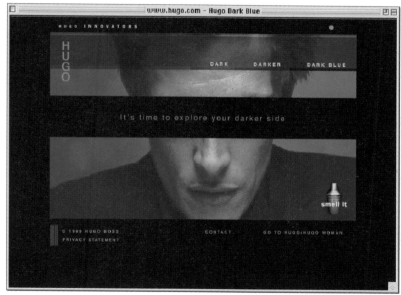

WWW.HUGO.COM/
ROMAN LUBA, MARTA SANT ET AL | PIXELPARK AG | WWW.PIXELPARK.COM   GERMANY

WWW.IRIS.DTI.NE.JP/~CANNO/

JAPAN

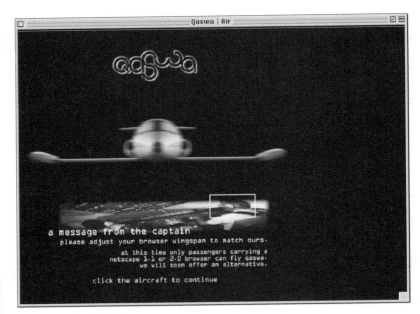

WWW.QASWA.COM/STANDARD.HTML

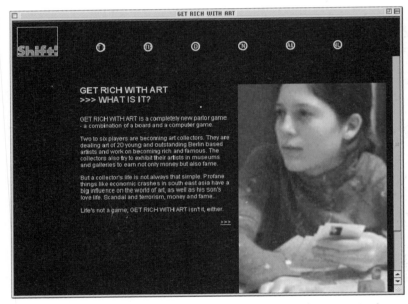

WWW.TRILLION.DE
FLORIAN THALHOFER | TH@LHOFER.COM

GERMANY

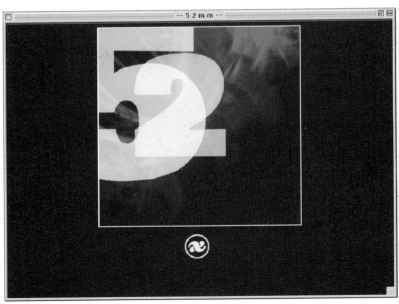

WWW.52MM.COM/
MARILYN DEVEDJIEV | 52MM | TYPEDIVA@52MM.COM

USA

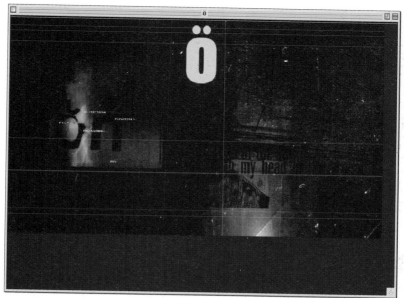

WWW.MENTALGRAVITY.COM
HENRIK BRINKS | WWW.AROS.DK

DENMARK

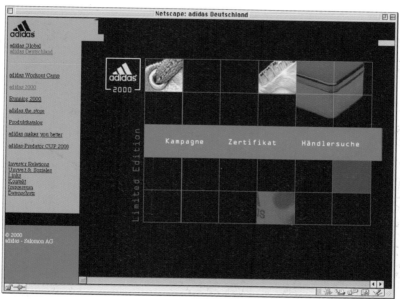

WWW.ADIDAS.DE/ADIDAS/CONCEPT2000/INDEX.HTML
JO WICKERT, HEIKE SAEHLBRANDT | PIXELPARK AG | WWW.PIXELPARK.COM

GERMANY

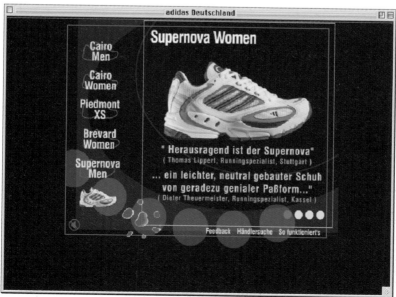

WWW.ADIDAS.DE/ADIDAS/RUNNING/RUNNING.HTML
JO WICKERT, HEIKE SAEHLBRANDT | PIXELPARK AG | WWW.PIXELPARK.COM

GERMANY

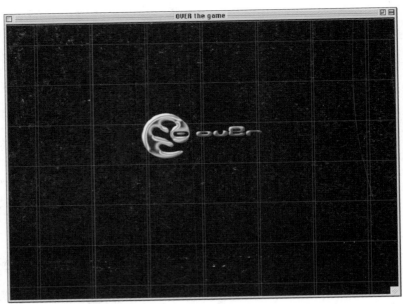

WWW.OVERTHEGAME.COM
JAUME PERIS, ORIOL GRANES, BRUNO BARRACHINA | QUIN TEAM! | WWW.QUINTEAM.COM   SPAIN

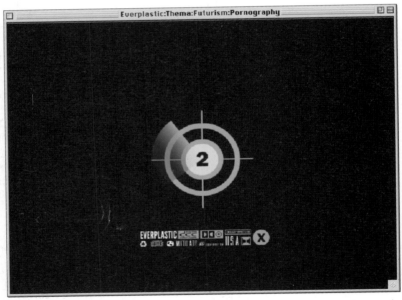

WWW.EVERPLASTIC.COM/DEFAULT.HTM
JIM MARCUS   USA

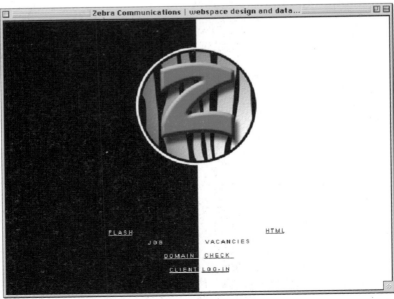

WWW.QUAY.CO.UK/~ZEBRA/ZEBRAD.HTM
WWW.ZEBRA.CO.UK   UK